Praise for

The Essential Workplace Conflict Handbook:

"The pragmatic solutions offered in *The Essential Workplace Conflict Handbook* help minimize the human drama inherent in conflict resolution, which inevitably strengthens the team. This book is a must-read."

—Mark A. Raitor, Chief Operating Officer,
Independent Community Bankers of America

"Barbara Mitchell and Cornelia Gamlem have done it again! In their latest book, *The Essential Workplace Conflict Handbook*, they explore the many facets of workplace conflict using practical examples. They provide terrific advice on exploiting as well as resolving it. Buy it, read it, rely on it, and you will never regret it!"

—Sarah Bowman Rajtik, PHR, Chief of Staff/
Director of Human Resources, The RSR Company

"Following their success with *The Big Book of HR*, Gamlem and Mitchell have produced another winner with *The Essential Workplace Conflict Handbook*. This practical, hands-on guide to managing workplace conflict should be on the bookshelf—and in the hands—of managers at all levels of organizations large and small."

—Ralph Kidder, Chief Financial Officer,
Marymount University (Retired)

"Having a productive and engaged workforce is an imperative for organizations to be successful. Leaders must be able to not only motivate their teams but they must also be able to deal effectively with conflict. In this book Cornelia and Barbara discuss the causes of conflict and they also provide clear suggestions for addressing each different situation. This is an excellent resource for anyone with 'people' responsibility."

—Janet Parker, SPHR, EVP, Corporate HR,
Regions Bank

"Cornelia Gamlem and Barbara Mitchell have another hit on their hands. They have identified the single most important issue resulting from workplace stress, and then told us how to effectively deal with it. Conflict management skills can be greatly enhanced using their new book. Every manager and supervisor in America should have their own copy dog-eared within a week."

—William H. Truesdell, SPHR, SHRM-SCP,
President, The Management Advantage, Inc.,
Co-author, *PHR/SPHR Certification Exam Guide*

"Conflict is inevitable in the workplace, and so often HR finds itself in the middle of conflict situations. *The Essential Workplace Conflict Handbook* contains real-life examples which are useful in resolving conflicts. Recognizing there are rarely 'one size fits all' solutions that satisfy all parties, the book covers a variety of topics. To address conflicts arising from the many changes in today's workplace the book discusses a scenario involving individuals from diverse backgrounds and generations, who grew up with different views, who must now work together.

A key topic also covered is managing expectations. While we expect adults in the workplace to act maturely, this is not always the case, and someone must step in to arbitrate. This handbook a valuable resource for HR professionals, managers, anyone involved in resolving workplace conflicts and I highly recommend its reading."

—Gus Siekierka, Vice President and Chief Human Resources Officer, CSC (Retired)

"*The Essential Workplace Conflict Handbook* is greatly needed in the American workplace. With cultural diversity, changes in demographics, and rapidly changing technology, I'm not sure how we've come this far without this masterpiece. The authors have clearly defined all aspects of conflict and the resolution thereof. A must-have for every office and workplace. It truly is ESSENTIAL!"

—Kathleen Zurenko, MCS, Adjunct Professor, Daytona State College

"Conflict in the workplace, while often stressful, can be the sign of a vibrant, creative, and engaged culture... especially when it arises from legitimately different views of how to proceed with something. The trick is how to leverage that tension to bring about the optimal solutions while retaining, and perhaps even developing inter-person and intra-team relationships. This book is a thoughtful and useful guide to not just 'conflict resolution' but what I call 'conflict optimization.' I highly recommend that everyone—not just leaders—read and benefit from it."

—Al Risdorfer, CHRO, Digital Divide Data

"Anyone who has ever encountered disruptive behavior at work must read *The Essential Workplace Conflict Handbook*. Cornelia Gamlem and Barbara Mitchell have done a great job deconstructing behavior types and explaining how to address that behavior before it escalates into something more serious. Workplace conflict need not become more complicated if people have the tools to confront it, and the authors have done just that."

—Arnold Sanow, Author, *Get Along with Anyone, Anytime, Anywhere*

"I'm all about results and *The Essential Workplace Conflict Handbook* is all about positive outcomes. Not only do Mitchell and Gamlem explore the root causes of many workplace conflicts, but their storytelling technique provides practical illustrations of conflicts that can occur in the workplace along with guidance for addressing and solving them. This book should be on the bookshelf for anyone who wants the ability to identify and resolve workplace conflict. The techniques you learn from this book will make you a better leader, co-worker and decision-maker."

—Angela Galyean, PHR, Vice President Human Resources, Intelsat

"Whenever a group of people come together at work, there are going to be differences. When there are differences, there's going to be conflict. Barbara Mitchell and Cornelia Gamlem do a great job of exploring these differences throughout the book as they show the readers how conflict can begin and ultimately be resolved. *The Essential Workplace Conflict Handbook* is a must-read for anyone who wants to move beyond conflict and on to respect!"

—Mary-Jane Sinclair, SPHR, President, Sinclair
Consultants, LLC

"In this comprehensive book, the authors provide readers with a wealth of information and stories to guide you through the often daunting world of workplace conflict. Mitchell and Gamlem are respected experts in HR and have generously shared their knowledge and experiences in this valuable new book. *The Essential Workplace Conflict Handbook* is useful, concise, and sensible."

—Sharon Armstrong, author of *The Essential
Performance Review Handbook*, *The Essential HR
Handbook*, and *Stress Free Performance Appraisals*

"Every workplace experiences conflict, and most organizations don't train employees, managers, or executives on how to resolve these issues successfully. If conflict isn't mitigated it will only prevent employees from reaching their fullest potential. This handbook provides valuable, practical tools for diagnosing the problem and resolving this disruptive behavior. I want all our managers and executives to read this book!"

—Gail Hyland-Savage, Chief Operating Officer,
Michaelson, Connor & Boul

"Connecting with your audience means you must understand their language. Drawing upon their own frontline experiences working with people, Gamlem and Mitchell have crafted a comprehensive yet practical reference for dealing with conflict in the workplace. *The Essential Workplace Conflict Handbook* is a valuable resource for anyone who wants to understand conflict at its core."

—Gerry Crispin, SPHR, Co-Founder, CareerXroads

"Conflict is a daily part of our professional lives. This resource, with its practical approach, will help us deal with it effectively and give us the confidence to handle it well. Thanks Barbara and Cornelia for another insightful handbook!"

—Deb O'Grady, Director, Training and
Development, Akima, LLC

"Readers will recognize many of the real-world examples from our own experiences and relish the essential tips on how to deal with them when we face them again. I expect many companies will make this a 'must-read' for their managers."

—Gary Cluff, President, Cluff & Associates

"*The Essential Workplace Conflict Handbook* hits all the key aspects of conflict in the workplace—from its causes to the steps that individuals and organization can and should take to resolve it. I hope everyone heeds the authors' call to properly diagnose the underlying issue before trying to solve it!"

—Tory Ruttenberg, Founder and President,
Ruttenberg Consulting, LLC

"Mitchell and Gamlem have structured and organized the complexities of workplace conflict in a manner that makes it accessible and usable. Each chapter can stand alone as a ready reference and job-aid to facilitate conflict resolution, from identifying root cause to skillfully engaging stakeholders in finding positive paths forward. This excellent work goes beyond a 'must-read' to a *must-use*. It will make a valuable addition to any HR practitioner's toolkit."

—Joseph P. Murphy, Vice President, Shaker Consulting Group, Inc

"*The Essential Workplace Conflict Handbook* lays a vivid, practical pathway for supervisors to manage, if not avoid, conflict within their organizations. It is a primer for managers who need to brush up on their team management skills and a handy reference for those who daily engage in conflict management. I strongly recommend this books for those who want to move beyond conflict and toward collaboration in their workplaces."

—Lee S. Webster, JD-MBA, SPHR, GPHR, Dir, Talent Acquisition and Recruitment, University of Texas Medical Branch

"Authors Mitchell and Gamlem have written a very timely book that deals with the inevitable conflicts in the workplace that arise and helps one chart a path on how to maneuver in this new world of complex organizations with its many diverse cultures, generational differences and work styles. Armed with checklists and an extremely relevant appendix, this book should be sitting on every manager's desk."

—Karen Bloom, Principal, Bloom, Gross & Associates, Inc

The Essential
WORKPLACE
CONFLICT
Handbook

THE ESSENTIAL
WORKPLACE
CONFLICT
HANDBOOK

A QUICK AND HANDY RESOURCE FOR ANY
MANAGER, TEAM LEADER, HR PROFESSIONAL,
OR ANYONE WHO WANTS TO RESOLVE
DISPUTES AND INCREASE PRODUCTIVITY

BARBARA MITCHELL AND CORNELIA GAMLEM
Authors of *The Big Book of HR*

CAREER
PRESS

Pompton Plains, N.J.

THE ESSENTIAL WORKPLACE CONFLICT HANDBOOK
EDITED BY ROGER SHEETY
TYPESET BY KARA KUMPEL
Cover design by Jeff Piasky
Printed in the U.S.A.

To order this title, please call toll-free 1-800-CAREER-1 (NJ and Canada: 201-848-0310) to order using VISA or MasterCard, or for further information on books from Career Press.

The Career Press, Inc.
12 Parish Drive
Wayne, NJ 07470
www.careerpress.com

Library of Congress Cataloging-in-Publication Data

Mitchell, Barbara, 1943-
  The essential workplace conflict handbook : a quick and handy resource for any manager, team leader, HR professional, or anyone who wants to resolve disputes and increase productivity / Barbara Mitchell, Cornelia Gamlem.
      pages cm
  Includes bibliographical references and index.
  ISBN 978-1-63265-008-5 (paperback) -- ISBN 978-1-63265-990-3 (ebook) 1. Conflict management. 2. Personnel management. 3. Leadership. I. Gamlem, Cornelia. II. Title.

HM1126.M58 2015
303.6'9--dc23

                                                     2015028907

This book is dedicated to my wonderful, supportive family and to a great group of friends who listen to me complain about deadlines and always offer encouragement. Thank you!

—Barbara Mitchell

This book is dedicated to my husband, Carl Gamlem; and my son, Erik Gamlem. To Carl, for staying out of my way during bursts of creative energy. To Erik, for growing up to be my creative sounding board. Thanks to you both for your unconditional love and support on this journey.

—Cornelia Gamlem

Acknowledgments

Writing a book is a journey and this journey began long before Career Press approached us with the idea. Throughout the courses of our respective careers, we have encountered people and situations that provided inspirations for the topics that we discuss in this book.

There are some people who made special contributions to this stop along this journey, people to whom we are especially grateful. Susan Devereaux is at the top of the list for her contribution. You edited and formatted the manuscript for us and helped to keep us on track. Thank you, Susan, for your patience, your insights, and your questions. Our colleague Sharon Armstrong deserves a special mention. You opened the door that allowed us to become writers and authors. Thank you, Sharon, for continuing to be our biggest supporter. Arnold Sanow gave us terrific advice and insight into the difficult and sadly emerging topic of workplace bullying. Thank you, Arnold, for your guidance. Thanks to our great colleagues in the BYOB Club (the second B stands for Books, not Booze!). We value your support, insights, and great stories. Maybe someday one of our books will make the reading list!

Thanks to Marilyn Allen, our literary agent, for her help, advice, and encouragement to "write on." And thanks to the staff at Career Press for continuing to believe in us. Special thanks to our editors, Kirsten Dalley and Roger Sheety. We appreciate all your support.

Finally, Cornelia would like to acknowledge the memory of my friend, Arlyce Robinson, who always knew when "I'm not in it!" (I refer the reader to Chapter 9 to understand this.) Arlyce, you're still an influence to the many lives you've touched. A special acknowledgment goes to Cornelia's siblings, Rosanne Andrews and Vincent Gibaldi, who first introduced me to conflict. Despite it all, I know you always had my back.

CONTENTS

Introduction

Conflict is neither good nor bad. Properly managed, it is absolutely vital.

—Kenneth Kaye

Conflict thrives in the world today. One only has to pay attention to current events to be convinced that we live in times when, if conflict doesn't exist, someone will find a way to disagree or disrupt whatever is happening. We wonder, "Why can't we all just get along?" Conflict in the workplace can be particularly stressful because your livelihood depends on workplace success.

As Lynne Eisaguirre says in *The Power of a Good Fight*, "The workplace continues to change at a rapid pace. Diversity, outsourcing, work group teams, and mergers between companies that used to be competitors increase workplace conflict. And yet, most of us lack a creative conflict approach. Most of us are afraid to embrace and harness the powerful force of conflict. We either run from it or create destructive disputes."[1]

Workplace conflicts tend to be between people—interpersonal conflict. Usually, conflict occurs between two or more people who see things differently or want to take the project or work in a different direction from where their colleague thinks it should go. Sometimes conflicts occur over resources when one project is allocated more money than another or when a coworker thinks someone else is taking credit for his/her work.

Sometimes conflicts take the form of bickering between the people involved and other times conflicts emerge when one coworker criticizes the work of another. At its worst, conflicts can result in verbally abusive situations. And then there are the situations where someone perceives there is a conflict, but in reality, it doesn't exist!

Conflicts may occur in the workplace due to differences in communication styles or may be related to people coming from diverse backgrounds. Conflicts certainly occur in times of change or when people are under pressure—whether real or perceived.

Is conflict intrinsically bad? Can there be good conflict? Certainly conflict is bad when it drains energy from the work that needs to be done or when it divides teams or workgroups. Conflict is bad when it is personally directed to others in the organization. However, conflict can be positive when it leads to creative problem solving and it can drive an organization to consider new possibilities in a highly competitive world.

Whether conflict works for or against an organization depends entirely on how workplace conflict is managed.

The Essential Workplace Conflict Handbook defines conflict as "a condition between or among workers whose jobs are interdependent; who are angry or frustrated; who perceive others to be at fault; or, who act in ways that cause an organizational problem."

Some people seem to enjoy conflict whereas others run from it and avoid it at all costs. Those who run from it may be fearful of being seen as negative for bringing up the issue or they may not have confidence in their ability to do anything about the issue. Or, they may just be more comfortable in having everyone get along even though they and all the rest of us know that isn't possible in the workplace or in life!

The Essential Workplace Conflict Handbook looks at some of the things that cause conflict, including organizational change, the impact of a diverse workforce, the role teams play in work today, technology, and globalization. (We cover these in detail in chapters 1–3.) We also give readers many resources to help ensure that conflicts can be managed and can, in fact, help drive the organization to higher levels of creativity and productivity. We offer help for tackling the most difficult workplace conflict challenges by providing information you can use right now to help you have a more creative and productive workplace.

This book gives readers guidance on diagnosing the problem because, quite frankly, until you really know what the issue is, solving it is just not going to happen. This involves learning how to ask the right questions and not jumping to quick conclusions or making easy assumptions before you have all the facts. We discuss this more specifically in Chapter 4.

We also present information on the value of good listening skills. Most of us are not good listeners; we listen only until it is our time to talk! Chapter 5, therefore, provides information on listening techniques, including active and reflective listening skills and the value of good dialogue.

We know that unmet expectations are the cause of many workplace conflicts, so in Chapter 6 we look at how to define roles and responsibilities so that employees know what is expected of them. We also look at the importance of accountability and at several leadership approaches to addressing conflict.

In order to resolve workplace conflicts, the parties involved have to focus on interests and not on positions. So in Chapter 7 we look at the differences between interests and positions, and the importance of focusing on interests rather than positions.

Until you know your own conflict type and the types of those with whom you work, you will have difficulty resolving workplace conflict. In Chapter 8, then, we discuss how to understand your own style and the style of others using an easy quiz. Once you understand the types, we give suggestions on how to maximize your own impact and how to work best with others who have types that are different from your own.

Another common misconception of problem solving is that resolutions must come from the top down. It's really not the job of the manager to get in the middle of any issue between employees. In fact, when the manager gets involved, employees don't learn how to manage conflict themselves. Chapter 9 discusses situations where conflict is present and it explores who owns the problem: Is it the manager, the employee, or both? We then describe situations in which a third party might be useful in resolving an issue and talk about the role of mediation in conflict resolution.

We devote Chapter 10 to looking at disruptive behavior and the negative impact it has on any organization or affected employees. We explore how behavior that begins as seemingly innocent can progress to harassment, bullying, or worse. We cover the importance of setting boundaries for workplace behavior and look at the concept of intent vs. impact.

In the last chapter, we give managers some suggestions of positive things that can be done that go beyond policies. There are many resources available to organizations, so we look at manager and employee training, Employee Assistance Programs, Workplace Flexibility Programs, wellness, and other ideas to help organizations deal with workplace conflict.

As you read *The Essential Workplace Conflict Handbook*, we believe it will become clear to you that now, more than ever, we need to find ways to manage conflict at work, and we sincerely hope this book will give you practical information for dealing with the inevitable conflicts you will face at work. Each chapter stands alone but, when applicable, we've included links to other chapters. We've included several resources in the Appendix such as links to Websites that you may find useful.

Our goal in writing this book was to acknowledge that workplace conflict exists at perhaps a higher rate than ever due to a wide variety of external and internal factors. We wanted to provide the reader with information, resources, and hope that conflict does not have to derail an organization; in fact, it can have a positive impact on creativity and productivity.

We wish you great success in managing any workplace conflict you encounter!

CHAPTER 1
WHAT'S NEW AT WORK?

If you don't like something, change it. If you can't change it, change your attitude.

—Maya Angelou

Let's start with the fact that just about everything is new at work these days. As the world economy shifts from day to day, jobs are lost and jobs are created with different skill set requirements. Each of us is being challenged to learn new technologies in order to build our skill sets and to help stay relevant in an increasingly technology-driven world.

As Sharon Armstrong says in *The Essential Performance Review Handbook,* "We're experiencing what *Future Shock* author Alvin Toffler might call 'an exclamation point in history,' an era in which old barriers fall and there is vast reorganization of the production and distribution of knowledge and the symbols used to communicate it."[1]

We now work in an increasingly global economy; so, in many organizations, competition is fierce to innovate and get new products to market as quickly as possible. And many organizations have been purchased or merged with international organizations, which has created a need for employees to change and adapt to new ways of doing business.

Managers were just getting used to dealing with four generations in the workplace when along comes the next one. And with the slower economy, many in the older generations have delayed retirements so that now many organizations are faced with having potentially five different generations working together. That can present major challenges and create stress that frequently results in conflict in the workplace. Although everyone in a particular generation may not see things like others in that generation, we know that there are generational differences in today's complex workplaces. The Millennial generation is coming into its own and will be the largest group of employees in the workplace in the next few years. This generation lives, eats, and breathes technology. Generation X and Millennials are taking leadership positions in organizations, which has the potential to create conflict when they are asked to manage people who are considerably older than they are. These changes can and will cause conflict!

➡Chapter 2: Why Can't Everyone Be Like Me?

Resisting change is futile. Change is everywhere and with it comes increasing chances for workplace conflict. Think about an organization that is in the process of being acquired by a competitor. Some employees adapt easily to the new organization whereas others want to hang on to the old ways of doing things. I once had a manager who said he felt like "everyone else was on the new boat moving down the river" while he "was stuck on the dock." He was unwilling to take the first steps to adapt to the new organization. His inability to move forward created huge conflicts in the organization because he was a key player. He didn't see that his resistance to change was creating major conflicts between him and those on his team who had already adapted to the new way of doing things required by the acquiring organization. He decided to leave the organization rather than adapt to the necessary changes. This is a rather drastic step to take, but it did resolve the conflicts created by his inability to modify his behavior.

The great thing about change in the workplace is that each of us has a choice as to whether to embrace it, resist it, or wait and see! Change can be managed to lessen the likelihood of conflicts, but let's not kid ourselves: Change does cause conflict, so all we can do is try to minimize it by managing the change effectively. We know that "organizations continually evolve, whether by expanding, contracting, exploring, or eliminating. Managers often joke that change is the one true constant in any organization, and it's undeniably true. Any organization that desires to improve or just keep up with its competitors has to change."[2]

Change is uncomfortable for many people. "Ruts, even the most boring and dull, are comfortable for us. We know the old tried-and-true ways are predictable, and what is new and different may be frighteneing."[3]

It's also a given that change can bring a whole new energy level to the organization. As soon as employees get on board with the change, things can happen that move the group, team, or department forward. The issue is how to get through the change and the conflicts that arise because of the change process and get on the other side! Managers must be on the lookout for conflicts that result from the desired changes to ensure the conflicts positively drive the changes the organization is seeking.

> "Consider the telephone...a rotary phone— a device created in 1918 that didn't change much for a half century. By contrast, there have been five versions of the iPhone in seven years."[4]

There are many changes that have the potential for creating conflict in the workplace. For example, consider:

✳ New leadership—a new CEO or executive director is named to an organization. No matter how hard he/she tries to instill confidence and to let the existing staff get to know him/her, this change can bring conflict out in the open.

Jim just retired from The Thomas Company after serving as CEO for more than 15 years. The organization didn't have a succession plan, so the board of directors used a well-known search firm to locate candidates to replace Jim. They selected Chad, who'd been COO of a competing company. Chad joined The Thomas Company three months ago and it hasn't gone well. Jim's management style was to hire good people and let them do their jobs, whereas Chad is much more of a "command and control" kind of leader.

Chad's direct reports are struggling to work together and some conflicts that would never have surfaced under Jim are now coming to the surface. The CFO and the VP of marketing are doing everything under the sun to undermine each other and it is obvious that Chad doesn't have a clue it is happening, so their conflict boils over into other parts of the organization.

⁎ Change in reporting relationships—what happens when an employee who has reported to one manager for 10 years is suddenly moved to another team?

Hal has been on the marketing team headed by his long time mentor and now personal friend, Ken. Through the years, they've developed a sort of shorthand when communicating with each other and the others on the team. Everyone knows they play golf every weekend when the weather cooperates and that their wives are best friends. A decision is made at the highest levels of the organization that Hal could make major contributions to the sales team and he is asked to now report to Wes. Hal and Wes know each other but have never liked each other. There is something about the other one's style that gets in the way of them working well together. Hal is also concerned that, after so many years of working closely with Ken, he doesn't really know as much as he should about the business and, now, Wes will find out and use that against him.

When Hal joins the sales team, he is unsure of himself and doesn't feel welcomed. The rest of the team have been operating as a well-functioning team for years and now this new person comes to their staff meetings. They've all known Hal through the years, but aren't sure about him. They are concerned that his relationship with Ken, his former boss, is too close and wonder whether he will tell Ken about all the issues they are facing. There has always been rivalry between the sales and the marketing teams and now they have to learn to trust Hal and find ways to work with him.

  ✳ New team member—a new hire is introduced
      to a group of people who've worked together
      for a long time; they don't know this person
      and he/she doesn't know them.

Celeste is hired away from a competing firm to join an existing group of coworkers who've been on the same team for many years. The team members read her bio when HR sends out the introductory e-mail, and though she has an impressive background and has been highly successful with the other company, they don't know her and don't trust her. Celeste comes in to a difficult situation—it is hard enough to start with a new firm, but she feels the pressure to prove herself as quickly as possible. To make matters even worse, she is replacing Tom, who had been on this team for more than five years and resigned to relocate when his wife took a job out of state. The team loved Tom and now Celeste is in his place.

  ✳ New technology/system—new software is in-
      troduced by your great IT team.

Cedric, head of IT, and his team hold classes to train everyone in the new system. They put together a Frequently Asked Questions document to help people adapt to the new system. They set up a help desk just for this implementation. Every effort is made by Cedric and his team to bring people up to speed on what they need to know, but many employees decide not to attend the training. The office is filled with gossip about how this is another major mistake; and, if they just hold on, maybe the company will go back to the old system. Cedric goes to the CEO to complain that he isn't getting the support he needs to make it happen, but the CEO really isn't interested in that level of detail and dismisses Cedric's concerns. The company has spent a lot of money on the new technology, but people are unhappy about it and unsure what it means for their jobs.

✳ Office redesign/relocation.

The Hyde Company has just moved into a beautiful new building. Before they moved, a team spent many hours working with the outside design team to come up with new ways of doing business. The old office space was dark and filled with long corridors. Everyone wanted a window office so that's what they had; even the administrative staff work stations had a window. This resulted in a very siloed office environment. There were no places for employees to get together except for the cramped coffee stations scattered around the office.

The new office design is totally different. It is open with very few walls. Even the offices along the windows have glass walls that can be moved or stored. The feeling is entirely different and collaborative.

Many employees openly hate the new office. They complain about the lack of privacy even though there are plenty of small rooms designed for privacy that anyone can use. Other people love it and think that it has really broken down the barriers between departments and they enjoy being able to meet with their co-workers in the huddle spaces set up around the building for collaboration.

✳ New policy or procedure.

A small nonprofit organization has received a lot of requests from staff members to telecommute a day or two a week. Martin, the executive director asked Lane, the chief of staff who had responsibility for HR issues, to research whether or not this was a good idea and if it was a good idea, how they could make it work for their organization. Lane gathered a few leaders in the organization to work with her on this. They surveyed other nonprofits and small businesses in their area and came up with a recommendation for how it would work. They announced it at a staff meeting and employees started working from home. There was a lot of confusion as to who was eligible and many upset employees when they asked their manager if they could telecommute and were told no without a reason. "If Sally can telecommute, why can't I?" became a frequently heard comment. Telecommuters were not given guidelines as to how they needed to be available at certain times during the day and what the expectation was as to how quickly they would respond to e-mails or voice mails. Rumors started when someone would call a telecommuter and get their voice mail—if that person wasn't available, it was obvious they weren't working. Of course, that was untrue as there are several legitimate reasons why a call goes to voice mail, including that the person may have been on the line with another co-worker solving a work-related issue.

✳ Fear of loss of job security.

Whyte and Associates has been a family-owned business since the current CEO's grandfather started the business in the 1960s. They have grown to more than 500 employees in three states, but their market share is diminishing. The leadership is evaluating all kinds of options to cut-costs and it is rumored that there will be layoffs. Productivity decreases as people fear for their jobs. There are several quiet meetings in the halls about whether or not to put a resume together and bail or wait to see what kind of severance packages are offered. Who is going to decide what jobs are safe and what jobs are eliminated? Trust in the leadership diminishes by the day.

✳ New responsibilities—even when the employee is excited about a promotion or additional responsibilities, it can be a time of high stress, which can create conflict.

Maya works for a large financial services firm. She's been there for five great years and her career progression is right where she wants it to be. She is expecting to be promoted to director in the next six months. She's called to her boss's office on a Monday morning and after they chat about their weekends, the boss tells her that her promotion will be sooner rather than later. Maya is excited, but apprehensive because she knows two of her peers were also hoping for this promotion. Her boss tells her that he has great confidence in her and will support her as she takes on the new responsibilities, but she is nervous about facing her co-workers, who may find ways to undermine her work.

✻ Colleague/friend resignation—employees, especially Millennials, want to have a good friend at work, so consider what can happen when the best friend resigns or, even worse, is terminated.

Sierra and Kaitlyn started work at the bank on the same day and became instant friends. They eat lunch together almost every day and share everything about their personal lives. They work in different departments; however, when the loan department is facing a downsizing and Kaitlyn's job is eliminated, Sierra is devastated. She begins to question her job at the bank and to resent the people in Kaitlyn's old department that survived the layoff.

✻ Loss of job freedom.

Ricardo and Dakari have been working at a large trade association where they had a lot of discretion with how they did their jobs and when they worked. The managers to whom they reported trusted them to complete their work on time and allowed them to have a flexible schedule to suit their personal and family needs. Dakari now reports to a new director who has eliminated any flex time, and he now has to be at this desk at 8 a.m. and can't leave before 5:30 p.m. Ricardo's department still allows flex time. Dakari is unhappy and takes it out on his former coworker rather than going to his manager to complain.

✻ Loss of pride in the organization.

Tenisha has worked for the Gilbert Company for more than 10 years and one of the reasons she joined them was because of the great work they do in the community. The company has been a strong supporter of local charities and she's been able to have some influence, which allowed her to put forward some of her favorite causes. A recent change in leadership has resulted in the company cancelling its commitment to several important charities in their small town. Tenisha still personally volunteers at those organizations and is embarrassed that her company has pulled its support. She is no longer proud to work for the Gilbert Company and has had several difficult conversations with her boss about how she feels. Her boss tells her not to make waves at this time, but to "ride it out" and see if things change. She now feels as if her boss doesn't understand her point of view and they've had a difficult couple of weeks.

Any of these changes we just described can cause conflict within organizations. As organizations change (and we know they will!), what steps can be taken to mitigate the number and severity of conflicts? Patrick Lencioni writes:

> When team members trust each another, when they know that everyone on the team is capable of admitting when they don't have the right answer, and when they're willing to acknowledge when someone else's idea is better than theirs, the fear of conflict and the discomfort it entails is greatly diminished. When there is trust, conflict becomes nothing but the pursuit of truth, an attempt to find the best possible answer. It is not only okay, but desirable. Conflict without trust, however, is politics, an

attempt to manipulate others in order to win
an argument regardless of the truth.[5]

When change occurs in any organization, managers must actively listen to what is being said about the change and do their best to understand where the root causes of the resistance to change are coming from. This is a time to over-communicate. Organizations need to use every means of communication possible and not overlook the rumor mill. Leaders can use the rumor mill to spread accurate information to counterbalance the negative information that will be spreading like wildfire in times of change. During times of change, there should be frequent meetings, e-mail blasts, and tweets to keep employees aware of what is happening and why. Savvy managers know how to effectively use every available communication method.

During times of change, it is more important than ever for managers to keep their commitments to their employees. In other words, do what you said you would do! In these periods, employees are especially tuned to what is promised and what is delivered, so don't let them down. It is always good management to be honest with employees, but it is even more critical in times of change.

Change initiatives can cause fears—whether founded or unfounded. Therefore, managers should respect the fears they see manifested in their people and take time to listen to their concerns. There is no way to totally overcome the fear of change, but keeping people informed, treating them with respect, and listening to them will go a long way toward getting you to where you want to be when the change process is completed.

If some employees are having a particularly difficult time adjusting to the changes in process, it may be a good idea to bring in some change management training and/or refer employees to your Employee Assistance Program for extra help.

Essential Tips

* ∗   Change is inevitable. It's how you handle it that matters!

* ∗   People react differently to change. Some embrace it quickly, whereas others resist or hold back to see how it plays out.

* ∗   Changes can cause conflict in organizations.

* ∗   Over-communicate during times of change.

* ∗   Use your good listening skills to keep in touch with your staff.

* ∗   Monitor employees closely to determine who might need extra help with the change.

CHAPTER 2

WHY CAN'T EVERYONE BE LIKE ME?

Cultural diversity and inclusion thrives when people with unique perspectives work together to achieve common goals.

—Candice Bernhardt

Diversity in the workplace really isn't anything new. The workforce of the past may have appeared homogeneous, but diversity was present. During the past several decades as society has become more mobile and workplace demographics have changed, we've become more aware of diversity. Beyond changing demographics, diversity includes those biological, physical, environmental, and cultural differences that differentiate us from others, and that distinguish us as individuals or groups of individuals.

Each of us possesses many unique characteristics that are often described as dimensions of diversity. There are primary or core dimensions—those dimensions that are unable to be changed and often visible to others. These are characteristics that we can't control and that have a powerful and sustained impact throughout our lives. They include age, ethnicity, gender, mental/physical abilities and characteristics, race, sexual orientation, and gender identity.

In addition to these core dimensions, there are secondary dimensions—characteristics over which we have control and are able to change, that are less visible to others, and that are more variable in the degree of influence they exert on our lives. They include:

* Education.
* Geography.
* Socio-economic status.
* Marital/family/parental status.
* Military experience.
* Religious beliefs.
* Work experience.
* Work/communication style.[1]

Diversity dimensions aren't the only things that differentiate and shape individuals. Also impacting our behavior are cultural dimensions or variables. Culture is the acquired knowledge people use to interpret experiences and generate behavior. Culture is shared by almost all members of social groups and is something older members of the group pass on to younger members. In addition to shaping behavior, culture structures our perception of the world—our attitudes, beliefs, and values.

Management consultants Fons Trompenaars and Charles Hampden-Turner identified seven dimensions of culture after 10 years of researching the preferences and values of people in different cultures around the world. Their findings were detailed and published in their book, *Riding the Waves of Culture.* They found that each culture has its own way of thinking, its own values and beliefs, and different preferences. What distinguishes one culture from the other is where these preferences fall on the continuum of each dimension that they identified:

* Rules vs. relationships.
* The individual vs. the group.
* How far people get involved.
* How people express emotions.
* How people view status.
* How people manage time.
* How people relate to their environment.

➡ Appendix: Seven Dimensions of Culture

Whereas Trompenaars and Hampden-Turner's research focused on cultures within countries or national groups, culture extends to other social groups. Think of the social groups to which an individual may belong such as a religious group, a professional group, the organization where he/she works, the department or team within the organization, and a book club or a group associated with a hobby, to name a few. The most basic social group of all is the family, and families come in all shapes and sizes. Each of these groups has its own distinct culture and variables within that culture. Beyond the dimensions identified by Trompenaars and Hampden-Turner, there are other variables that run along a continuum that may be observed within a particular culture or social group. These can include, but aren't necessarily limited to:

* Problem-solving style (linear/logical vs. lateral/intuitive).

* Communication style (direct vs. indirect).

* Extrovert vs. introvert.

* Approach to change (change oriented vs. tradition oriented).

* Approach to conflict resolution (confrontation vs. harmony).

➡ Chapter 8: What's Your Type?

Consider some of the following diversity dilemmas that can occur in the workplace:

It was frustrating for Gloria whenever she had to have a conversation with Veena, an associate on her team. Veena always looked down at her shoes and never looked Gloria in the eye. Gloria would wonder if Veena was engaged in the discussion and understood what she was saying. Worse, she was wondering if Veena was hiding problems about the assignment from her. What Gloria didn't understand was that Veena came from a culture that believed that less eye contact is more respectful. Because Gloria was the team leader, Veena was merely showing her respect.

Kate and Jack are part of a team that develops products for clients. Kate is an engineer on the design side of the team and product excellence surpasses all other considerations. Jack, on the other hand, is part of the sales team and is always eager to close the deal. Relationships surpass all other considerations and he's out to please. He'll promise the customer that the company can make any design change requested and then advise Kate what has to be done. The two often end up having heated discussions!

Sarah, a fairly recent college graduate, feels as if she is expected to carry the workload for her department—two coworkers and the manager. Her two coworkers, both of whom are parents of small children, frequently take personal days and leave early because of family obligations. When she recently asked to leave early to attend to something, her manager denied the request saying that the project needed to be finished that night and she was the only one who could stay late. Sarah had promised her cousin that she'd look in on her 85-year-old mother, Sarah's aunt, while her cousin was out of town on a business trip. The manager assumed Sarah had no family obligations because she was single. Sarah is now beginning to resent her coworkers.

An organization recently changed to a business-casual dress code, a change that was embraced by most of the staff. Jorge overhead this remark in the hallway about his team members: "They are so arrogant. They think they're superior to the rest of us with the way they walk around in their suits all the time." What the critic didn't realize was that members of Jorge's team were often called to unscheduled, external meetings where business attire was expected.

Barry, a finance director, was listening intently as Michaela was talking about her company's experiences moving to a shared services model where each division would receive support services from a centralized department, rather than have separate HR or accounting departments in each division. When she started talking about the cost savings achieved, Barry's face lit up. Michaela, who spent her career in HR and organizational development, saw his expression and immediately said, "But I'm very worried about the people in our shared services unit. We've cut staff to the minimum and expect much more work from them. I'm concerned that they are going to burn out." Barry began to object when Michaela reminded him that there are costs associated with burnout, starting with turnover. Barry was looking solely at the metrics and the costs. Michaela understood those issues, but was also concerned with the people side of the business.

Differences Matter

Although diversity may have always existed in the work force, its nature and extent continue to change dramatically. The U.S. Bureau of Labor Statistics reports statistics about the U.S. labor force that includes demographic characteristics from the Current Population Survey (CPS). The statistics provide information regarding gender, race and ethnicity, disability, education attainment, family and marital status, foreign-born workers, veterans, age, and older workers.[2]

Generational differences are a big force in today's workplace. We will soon have five generations in the U.S. workforce: Traditionalists, Baby Boomers, Generation Xers, Millennials, and now the Internet generation, who are on the cusp of making their entry. Each generation brings its own experiences and points of reference, leaving many to wonder:

* ❋ Do employees understand how work is done differently in different generations?

* ❋ Do employees understand customer needs, interaction, and work styles from different generations?[3]

> A retirement-eligible veteran teacher explains to an *Education Week* writer why she is still on the job with no intentions of retiring by describing her assets as a teacher leader: "I teach alongside colleagues who are younger than my own children.... They have energy and technology skills that I do not, but I have pedagogical skill and experience that I can share and that they want. I am a trusted sounding board and a source of institutional knowledge to my younger principal...."[4]

Each of us sees and experiences the world differently. We and a coworker are often presented with the same information. We take in that information—what we see and hear—and process it. We are going to notice certain things about the information and our coworker is going to notice different things about the same information. We each pay attention to different things.

After we've processed the information, we interpret it, give it meaning, and draw conclusions. However, our coworkers interpret the same information differently using their experiences, values, individual diversity, and cultures, and potentially draw a different conclusion. We each give the same information context by drawing on our own past experiences. As information is processed and interpreted, it can be given a different meaning by different people leading to different conclusions being drawn.[5] Different stories will emerge.

> **Avoid this pitfall:** Language is not universal. Different words and phrases can have different meanings to different people. Clarify and check for understanding.

Stereotypes, Socialization, and Assumptions

A stereotype is an over-generalized belief that is affixed to all members of some identifiable group (think dimensions of diversity and culture). A stereotype is biased material that may have been the basis of our socially constructed reality—our truth. In the worst case, when we are unaware of our biases, stereotypes can be fixed and inflexible notions about a group that blocks our ability to think about people as individuals. Many of these generalizations are based on misconceptions and errors in judgment and they are often disrespectful. Nevertheless, stereotypes and biases remain a constant part of our everyday thinking. Consider a time when someone made an assumption about you based solely on one of your dimensions of diversity. Then think about how it made you feel!

We develop stereotypes through socialization—the process through which we learn how to act according to the rules and expectations of a particular culture. Keep in mind that we are each part of many different cultures or social groups.

Socialization is the way we learn to perceive our world: how to interact with others, how to act in certain circumstances, and what our culture or social group defines as good and bad, right and wrong. Socialization allows a group to create members whose behaviors, desires, and goals correspond to those considered appropriate and desirable by the group. For example, physicians take the Hippocratic Oath to do no harm. That oath forms the basis of their behaviors in the medical profession. Through socialization, the needs of the group become the needs of the individual.

The bottom line is that when stereotypes form the basis of our belief system, they lead us to assumptions that get in the way of our ability to lessen tension, address conflict, and solve problems.

> Research by a leader in the field of hidden bias shows that the human brain is wired to make lightning-quick decisions that draw on one's assumptions and experiences, but that may also be based on misguided generalizations.[6]

Rachel and Alex are project managers. Monica, a new associate, has been assigned to work with both of them. When it's time for performance appraisals, both Rachel and Alex are asked to provide input to their director about Monica's performance. They are on opposite ends of the spectrum in their thinking. One example is that Rachel gives Monica very high ratings for her organizational skills whereas Alex rates her much lower. Rachel protests and provides an example of Monica's work product, which has summarized and arranged data in charts and graphs. Alex replies that he always has to request that things be done over because the material Monica produces for him is never clear. On further probing, their director learns that the difference lies not in Monica's work, but in Rachel's and Alex's approaches. Rachel has taken the time to show interest in Monica and explains the nature and scope of the project as well as the work product she expects from each assignment. Alex, on the other hand, believes that Monica should take the initiative to learn about the project on her own, just as he did, and merely leaves her written instructions via e-mail.

One of the reasons Rachel and Alex have a different story to tell about Monica is that they have vastly different backgrounds. Rachel was raised in a supportive, nurturing family whereas Alex's parents were distant and aloof. Their individual backgrounds have shaped their work style and influence their perspectives of Monica's performance.

Different perspectives and interpretations are normal and not necessarily good or bad. Problems and conflicts arise when we become blind to things outside our prism and experiences. If we believe our view is right and all others are flawed, we become blind to opportunities and possibilities.[7]

Rachel and Alex will continue to have a difficult time agreeing about Monica's performance until they recognize the noise that's hindering their communication—noise or barriers that are hindering the receiver (let's say Alex) from getting the message that the sender (Rachel) intended, and the reverse. This noise includes the dimensions of diversity and culture discussed earlier. Rachel and Alex have to recognize the barriers as a cause of their communication problem and work to overcome it.[8] They have to get rid of the noise by identifying the lenses and filters that distort the message.

➡ Appendix: Barriers to Communication

Beyond Two Stories

In order for Rachel and Alex to move forward, they each must get past the belief that their view is right and that the other is wrong. Getting past that belief is a process for everyone, a process that will take some time, understanding, and patience.

> Do not believe in anything simply because you have heard it. Do not believe in anything simply because it is spoken and rumored by many. Do not believe in anything simply because it is found written in your religious books. Do not believe in anything merely on the authority of your teachers and elders. Do not believe in traditions merely because they have been handed down for many generations. But after observations and analysis, when you find that anything agrees with reason and is conducive to the good and benefit of one and all, then accept it and live up to it.
>
> —Buddha

First, each person needs to understand how their individual story was shaped, and recognize that their past experiences led them to develop implicit rules by which they live their lives and construct their truths or beliefs about the world around them—in other words, how they were socialized. For example, Rachel, who was raised in the nurturing environment, believes that everyone should take an interest in and help to develop new associates. Alex believes that people should show independence and take initiative, and that they are responsible for their own development. Both people need to examine their own pasts, their implicit rules, and their own beliefs.

In examining your individual story, it's important to recognize that some or many parts of your own knowledge base may have faulty data—data that you may have been given throughout your life. It's helpful to ask yourself:

* Where did I learn that?
* Was the source credible?
* Have I been exposed to different perspectives?
* Am I wrong?
* Am I willing to step out of my comfort zone and grow?[9]

Understanding your own story prepares you for the next step: understanding the other person's story. This takes some courage because it involves having a crucial conversation with the other person, the type of conversation that is often difficult. As unpleasant as these conversations are, they are necessary to bridge the gap between what we think we know and what we actually know, the gap between where we are on the continuum of any of the cultural variables discussed earlier and where the other person is. We have to be willing to develop the skills that will allow us to temporarily suspend our beliefs and worldviews in order to entertain the beliefs and worldviews of others in a non-judgmental manner. We have to be willing to accept that our socially constructed reality—our truth—may not be the only truth and, in fact, it may be wrong.[10]

➡ Chapter 4: What's the Problem?
➡ Chapter 5: Listen Up!

The goal of having these conversations is to learn more about the other person so you have an opportunity to stand in their shoes. If Rachel could pretend for a moment that she were Alex, tried on his point of view and felt about Monica's performance the way he felt, it could bring her to a different level of understanding. Consider the experiences, realities (your truths), and background that you are bringing to the issue and contemplate what information you're missing about the other person. Ask the other person:

* Can you say a little more about how you see things?

* What information might you have that I don't?

* How do you see it differently?

* Can you say a little more about why this is important to you?

* How are you feeling about this situation?[11]

Respectful Curiosity

Respect is critical in all human interactions. Respect is dignity—giving positive attention to another person, listening to them, and acknowledging them whether you agree or disagree with their opinions or points of view. Respect is giving value to the other person as a human being, just as you would like them to give value to you. Respect provides the opportunity to look again with attention—to recognize the person, not just the different opinion. When we respect the other person, we look past the differences that may have kept us from fully seeing and understanding them. We look past the barriers and noise and give the other person the chance to be seen and to be heard.[12]

As you become curious, don't forget that people communicate differently. Some people have a direct style of communication, whereas others have a roundabout way of sharing information. An extrovert may be more open and forthcoming about her background and personal life than an introvert. However, another extrovert may wish to separate work from her personal life, not realizing how relationships impact work objectives. An introvert, on the other hand, may overlap between work and personal life because he believes that good relationships are necessary for all aspects of his life. These differences contribute to the difficulty of critical conversations.

One way to begin these conversations is to share something about yourself. You expose some of your own vulnerability by doing so and lay a foundation for asking questions. Rachel might start a conversation with Alex talking about her family—describing family gatherings and explaining how close her immediate (parents and siblings) and extended family (aunts, uncles, cousins) were to each other, and how they could count on each other in times of need. Even if Alex doesn't offer information, it might be easier for her to ask him some questions now that she's shared information. She might learn that he was an only child and that he was raised in a geographic area away from any relatives or that his family relocated often. This information could help both of them understand their own and the other's work style and reframe their conversations about Monica's performance.

Personal Initiatives

Fortunately, not everybody in the workplace is the same. How boring that would be! The variety of differences that exist in today's workforce present opportunities and challenges for everyone: employees, managers, and HR professionals. There are steps everyone can take to learn to appreciate and respect everyone with whom they work:

* Be authentic and find ways of communicating that allows yourself to be known and get to know others.

* Model behavior that includes respect for others, their opinions, interests, perceptions, values, experiences, and culture.

* Address differences and misunderstandings with a commitment to learning and resolving disagreements in a respectful and timely way.

* Communicate clearly, directly, and honestly.

❊ Encourage others to share their thoughts and experiences, and accept their frame of reference.

❊ Be willing to confront errors in judgment when you've relied on stereotypical thinking.

➡ Appendix: Diversity Self-Assessment Planner

Essential Tips

❊ Diversity in today's workforce is multi-dimensional and complex.

❊ Our individual diversity makes us unique and influences how we see the world and interpret information.

❊ Successful problem solving requires everyone to look past their biases and stand in the other person's shoes to see the issue from their perspective.

❊ Challenge your assumptions.

❊ Respectful curiosity and regular dialogue can lead to recognizing, respecting, and reconciling differences.

CHAPTER 3

WHAT'S HAPPENED TO
TEAM SPIRIT?

*Teamwork is the ability to work together toward
a common vision, the ability to direct individual accomplishment toward organizational objectives. It
is the fuel that allows common people to attain un-
common results.*

—Andrew Carnegie

We all pretty much know what a team is. We
learned about teams early on in school or in the
context of a sport. In fact, we talk more about
teams in a sports context than in any other. But,
according to Patrick Lencioni in *The Advantage*,

"Teamwork is not a virtue. It is a choice—and a strategic one."[1]

Now more than ever, work in the knowledge economy is frequently done by teams. The big difference between a work team and a sports team is at work, the team doesn't come together to try to beat an opponent—a team comes together to cooperate, pool their talents, and accomplish a particular set of tasks or responsibilities. In other words, teams have to work together to get the job done. And, because teams are made up of people, they can have conflict!

Most of us have been raised to be independent. We are well conditioned to be individualists—someone who can stand alone without a lot of support. Schools reward students for individual achievements and we learn early that, to get the best grades or to get into the best universities, we have to work hard and compete against other students for what we want. This continues into the workplace when we compete with other applicants for the jobs we want.

Now, at work, we're being told we have to be on a team. For some of us, this comes as a real shock. For example, until fairly recently, most young girls and women didn't play competitive sports, so they didn't have the team experience a lot of boys and men have. This can be a difficult transition when we have to think about the entire team and what part we play in the success of the task the team is undertaking. No longer are we competing with our peers; we are cooperating, and this can be a difficult transition to make and potentially cause conflicts in the workplace.

There are several different reasons we come together to work on a team. It might be to design a new product or a new service. It could be to solve a problem or it just might be to produce a product. Whatever the reason, working in teams can be a challenge for any organization, and it is important to take deliberate action to identify and remove barriers to effective teamwork.

➡ Appendix: Examples of Team Conflicts

As we discussed in Chapter 1, some people don't like things to change. They are pleased with the way things are and see no reason to do things differently. Some of these people may resent having to work on a team, whereas others may give the impression they like working on a team, but hold back from actively supporting it. Some team members may hold unrealistic expectations about the success of the team and when things don't go well (and there always will be times when things don't go well!), they may become dissatisfied and push back on the team thus causing conflict.

The Jones Company just signed an important new client. The CEO decided to form teams to develop strategies for working with the new business. He decided to not have each department work on just a specific part of the business; rather, he wanted to have cross-functional teams made up of people from each department. He didn't put a whole lot of thought into who should be on which team; he simply directed each of his vice presidents to pick a team and get started. He approached the team concept like it was a playground game.

As the teams began to meet, it was clear they weren't sure what their role was or what they were to accomplish, so they just stopped meeting and went back to their normal jobs. The VPs weren't sure what their role was either, so they weren't able to provide the necessary direction. No one had the courage to go to the CEO for guidance and the new client work was less than productive.

In order to be successful, teams need a clear direction in which to head; they need to have a focus, a purpose, and to know what is expected of them. Unclear expectations can derail even the strongest team and cause conflicts to occur. If a team has a clear vision of what they are expected to accomplish and they take the time to develop how they will work together, conflicts can be held to a minimum. But remember: Teams are made up of people, and where there are people, the potential for conflict exists!

➡ Chapter 6: You Want Me to Do What?

Setting goals for the team—whether it be for a project, a product, or any other purpose—can make a huge difference in the team's ability to accomplish their mission with as little conflict as possible. Use the SMART goal formula to help you craft team goals that will drive the team to success.

SMART Goals

S=Specific—a goal needs to be well defined and focused. Think about "who, what, why" and it will help you to be specific.

M=Measureable—how will you determine success for this goal? What measures do you need either short-term or long-term to measure success? Remember: "What gets measured gets done."

A=Achievable—nothing is more de-motivating than having a goal that is out of reach. Be sure the goal is achievable, but also a stretch. You want it to be a challenge, but not impossible.

R=Relevant—a goal should be linked to your organization's or team's current work or project.

T=Time-bound—a goal should have a date or time attached to it to ensure completion.

After the team gains clarity on their goals and objectives, it is critical that they come together to determine how they will work together. How often will they meet? Who will take notes? Who will chair the meetings? Where will reports be sent and when? These questions, and many others, need to be answered before a team can be effective.

Cynthia is always late for every team meeting. During the meetings, Juan whispers to his colleague. Larry spends all of his time on his phone responding to e-mails, while Leonard angles his chair so that his back is to most of the other team members. Lavinia leaves the meeting and shares whatever was discussed with her best friend at work.

Setting group norms is one way to minimize conflict when working in teams. Take the time at the beginning to set the "team norms"—how we are going to work together. The time invested in setting norms can pay off down the road and help the team be more collaborative and more effective.

The best way to set the team norms is to have a facilitator work with the team and come to consensus. Here is an example of team norms:

❊ Team members—we value differences and honor each member of the team for what he/she brings to the team. We create opportunities for each team member to learn and grow. We demonstrate flexibility. We share team norms with new team members.

✳ Deadlines—each team member agrees to make every effort to meet assigned deadlines and, if not possible, let the other team members know at least 48 hours in advance of the deadline that an extension is required.

✳ Meetings—we will rotate facilitation responsibilities in alphabetical order. The facilitator is responsible for collecting items for the agenda, preparing the agenda, distributing the agenda 24 hours in advance of the meeting, and keeping the discussions on target during the meeting. Meetings will start and end on time. All electronic devices will be turned off unless being used by a record keeper to take notes or by participants to follow the agenda. Unless there is an emergency situation (fire, natural disaster, illness), no one will leave a meeting until it is over.

✳ Record keeping—each meeting or update session will have a record keeper to take notes. Notes will be shared with other team members within 48 hours of the meeting.

✳ Confidentiality—all team activities will be held in confidence unless approval is given by the team leader.

✳ Decision-making—decisions will be made by consensus. When there is no consensus, the team can request a member of the Leadership Team to mediate until consensus is reached.

✳ Participation—all team members commit to being active in every way while a member of this team. This includes attending meetings and actively participating in discussions, completing assignments on time, and supporting other team members inside and outside meetings and projects.

✳ Roles—team leaders will be selected based on area of expertise and rotated based on project. Record keepers and facilitators will rotate in alphabetical order.

✳ Conflict resolution process—when we have different opinions on project issues, we will call a special session to listen to all points of view and work to understand each other's perspective before resolving the issues. If outside help is needed, we will request it.

✳ Accountability—each team member is fully accountable for all decisions made.

✳ Mutual respect—each team member agrees to respect the opinions and ideas of others. We will structure meetings to allow for each team member to have a voice equally.

Today's workplace is made up of people from all parts of the world with a variety of perspectives and work experiences. As reported in *Diverse Teams at Work*:

Whether the numerous diversities your team reflects center on distinctions such as work experience and position in the organization, cultural dissimilarities involving language and ethnicity, or some of the less changeable diversities such as age and race, one thing is clear. The way these differences are managed within the group will have tremendous consequences on how the team functions, and, ultimately, on how faithful it is to the accomplishment of its performance objectives.[2]

➡ Chapter 2: Why Can't Everyone Be Like Me?

Although diverse teams may seem like something new in organizations, they really aren't. But it makes sense to consider the importance of having a diverse team and to work to minimize potential conflicts on the team that may result from people coming from differing perspectives. Working with diversity on teams is a great place to reinforce one of the principles Stephen Covey laid out in *The Seven Habits of Highly Effective People*: "Seek first to understand—then to be understood."[3]

As described in *Diverse Teams at Work*, "Diversity Variables that Impact Team Functioning" include:

✳ "A teammate nods and says he understands, and then proceeds incorrectly.

✳ A coworker talks on and on, never getting to the point.

✳ A team member won't tell you when there is a problem.

✳ Some group members never speak out in meetings to make suggestions, yet you know they have some good ideas.

* A colleague pretends everything is fine, when you know she's upset.

* One member of the group comes unglued when meetings don't start on time."[4]

How inclusive is your team?

* Does your team value each member for what he/she brings to it?

* Do you foster open communication where every team member's voice is heard?

* Do you seek out opinions from everyone on the team rather than listening only to a few?

* Do you treat each other with respect and dignity?

* Do you find ways to celebrate your differences?

* Do team members mentor others in inclusive behaviors to build team competency?

* Do you provide resources to your team members on what inclusiveness means?

When issues come up on a team, it is important to try to diagnose whether the issue is due to a personality conflict or a communication breakdown that might be a result of some team members not understanding jargon or American slang or idioms.

When working in a team environment, it is critical to watch out for people who cause conflict, including:

* A team member reacts negatively if asked a question or to clarify a point.

* A team member loves to argue each point made; he/she is the "devil's advocate" on your team.

* A team member who loves to tell the leader or anyone how to do it better.

* A team member who just has to solve everyone else's problems.

In order for ideas to be presented and heard by the team, when team members are presenting ideas to each other, it is important that they:

* Maintain eye contact.

* Speak clearly in a loud enough voice to be heard and vary the pitch.

* Are sincere.

* Are energetic and engaging.

* Use animation such as gestures.

* Are positive and use positive language.

* Keep remarks brief but complete.

* End with a call to action and outline the next steps.

> The brainstorming process:
>
> * Decide on how long you have.
> * Set the ground rules such as:
>   o There is no bad idea—just get ideas flowing.
>   o Everyone must participate.
>   o You will get all ideas out before discussing them.

> ○ Consider using flip charts around the room for each person to record his/her ideas.
>
> ○ Anyone can piggyback on someone else's ideas.
>
> When you have your ideas, clarify, eliminate, consolidate, look for themes, evaluate, vote on the best, and move forward. Determine who will be the leader and who will be on which team and when the team will report back.

➡ Chapter 7: Don't Draw a Line in the Sand!

Whenever you ask people to work in teams, you are looking for them to come together to work on projects or issues that need resolving. When people work together in teams, you want to have conflict. Yes, that's what I said—you want conflict! You really don't want people thinking the same way, or agreeing just to agree, or to make someone else happy. As your team comes together to work on whatever their task, you really do want them to bring up different points of view and that may result in conflict. And that is a good thing because conflicts can spark innovation, provide a better solution, and make your team even stronger as you work through the conflict. Conflict can be positive for teams. Fear of conflict can derail a team. Good conflict can be about ideas, where people trust each other and where people know they can't have all the answers.

Team conflicts can happen over different approaches to the same issue or from personality conflicts or turf struggles. Trust allows conflict to be positive. You can work through the conflict to get to the best answer if there is trust. Very few people are unable to support a coworker just because they had a different idea.

In order for teams to work well together and to minimize conflict, there has to be trust among the members of the team. Teams thrive on mutual trust, so it is critical that trust be established as early as possible in the team's lifecycle. This sounds like a given, right? It's easy to say and sometimes not easy to do, but here are some ways to establish trust as soon as possible.

Talk about it in the first team meeting. By bringing the trust issue out in the open, you have a better chance of making it happen. "When there is trust, conflict becomes nothing but the pursuit of truth, an attempt to find the best possible answer."[5]

Pat Lencioni in *The Advantage* says, "The kind of trust that is necessary to build a great team is what I call vulnerability-based trust. This is what happens when members get to a point where they are completely comfortable being transparent, honest, and naked with one another, where they say and genuinely mean things like 'I screwed up,' 'I need help,' 'Your idea is better than mine,' 'I wish I could learn to do that as well as you do,' and even, 'I'm sorry.'"[6]

Be open and transparent. Teamwork and secrecy can't exist together, so be honest with the team and the team leadership. The team leader should model this behavior and not allow others to keep secrets or work behind the scenes without reporting back to the team. As team leader, try to:

✳   Share your vision for the team, the project, and the organization with your team members to give them a clear picture of where you're headed. Give clear direction and do your best to keep things on track.

* Get to know each team member as an individual. Learn what motivates each one and what frustrates each one.

* Communicate as often as possible and use a variety of communication methods. Be sure that each team meeting is documented and shared with the team. Work to cascade communication throughout the team so that everyone hears the same thing. Encourage a free flow of communication between team members.

* Encourage ideas and don't discount contributions from others on the team. It is easier for people to be creative in a team environment, so encourage new ideas and brainstorming.

* Acknowledge cultural differences when building trust. U.S.-based teams, for example, may be more trusting and comfortable than teams with members from other countries where it may take more time to build rapport.

* Acknowledge successes from everyone on the team. Trust will break down quickly if the team leader takes credit for something someone else contributed.

* Always treat team members with respect. Everyone on the team has a purpose and a value. Keep that in mind when conflicts arise!

* Remember: If problems come up, focus on the problem and not the person.

Daniel Goleman says in his landmark book, *Working With Emotional Intelligence*, "In a study by The Center for Creative Leadership of top American and European executives whose career derailed, the inability to build trust and lead a team was one of the most common reasons for failure."[7]

Here are some things to remember about teams from *The Essential Manager's Handbook*:

A team member is still an individual and should always be treated as such.

Cross-functional teams offer people the chance to learn about the roles and work of others.

Inter-departmental teams break down costly barriers.

Formal teams sometimes need informal elements to stimulate and refresh their work.

Teams cease to be teams if one member becomes dominant.

All team members should make sure they are working toward the same goals.[8]

As we've said many times in this book, conflict is a normal part of life, be it at work or at home. Conflict is not the sign of a mismanaged team; it is a reality of people working together. If a team is working well together, conflict is an indication that differences are acknowledged and are being dealt with. When there is conflict on your team, bring it to the surface in as non-threatening a manner as possible and ask the team members to identify the issues. When teams routinely handle conflict in this way and survive, odds are they will be comfortable when another issue arises. They will see that this is just a part of working on a team and move forward!

Essential Tips

* Most of us work in teams, so we need to learn how teams work.

* Use the SMART goal formula to set and monitor goals.

* Set group norms to ensure your team works well together.

* Try to have people from diverse backgrounds and ideas on your team; be inclusive.

* Use brainstorming to drive idea generation.

* Watch for people who cause conflict on your teams.

* You can't have a successful team without trust.

CHAPTER 4

WHAT'S THE PROBLEM?

Your assumptions are your windows on the world. Scrub them off every once in a while, or the light won't come in.

—Isaac Asimov

Consider the following situation: A customer follows up on a request for feedback at a local eatery because his order came out wrong. Somehow the ingredients in his omelet and his wife's got mixed up. He sends an e-mail to the owner, who wasn't in the restaurant when they visited, explaining what they ordered and what they received, attaching a copy of the receipt that detailed the order. A short time later, the owner sends a heartfelt apology along with an offer of a gift certificate for the customer's next visit and inquires, "Was the cashier who took your order male or female? I'll bet it was a female because she's new. We'll certainly go over things with her so she does not make the same mistake again."

This is so wrong on so many levels. First, the cashier was a male, someone who'd been working there for years. Second, as best the customer could tell from the receipt, the order was placed correctly and it was the kitchen staff that made mistakes. One of the items ordered was a breakfast special, an omelet with Swiss cheese. The omelet the customer received contained cheddar cheese. The receipt clearly showed that the breakfast special was ordered.

This was a teachable moment for the owner. She made an assumption, jumped to a conclusion, and had already assigned blame without examining all the evidence and gathering all the facts. She may have been creating conflict rather than managing it.

Problem solving is central to managing conflict, but the problem can't be solved until it's identified. Just like a physician must diagnose an ailment before treating it, so must parties to a conflict acknowledge that there is a problem and work to get to its source. No matter with whom you are in conflict—your boss, your coworker or teammate, your employee (if you're in a manager or leadership role), a peer—acknowledging and solving the problem is critical to assuring a positive organizational culture. Equally important is ensuring you are identifying, addressing, and solving the correct problem.

➡ Chapter 11: What's An Organization to Do?

What's in it for me? Resolving conflict empowers managers and employees to:

* Work effectively as teams.
* Build trusting relationship.
* Foster creativity.
* Contribute to the organizational knowledge.
* Confront destructive behavior and move to positive solutions.
* Take ownership and be a part of the solution.
* Build communication skills.
* Build consensus.

Conflict in organizations can often be good, and with a good conflict, relationships matter and are valued. Why do relationships matter? Flatter organizations and wider spans of control have dispersed power in organizations, giving lower-level managers and employees greater autonomy to take action and make decisions. With power dispersed, people need to negotiate solutions to problems with others, often those over whom they may have little or no formal authority.[1] Regardless of where you sit in an organization, you have a responsibility, as does everyone else, to maintain positive working relationships and problem solving is critical to those relationships.

Getting to the root cause of the problem requires an emphasis on fact finding and asking good questions.

Effective conversations and dialogue are keys to getting the facts and uncovering the problem.

> Claire is on a weekly conference call with a client and other members of the project team, some of whom work for other organizations. Claire is providing her update when her new boss, Jacob, walks into her office without knocking. He starts pacing back and forth and, finally, pulls a chair next to her and mutters under his breath how "pissed" he is. Obviously, it's his expectation that his presence trumps anything else that Claire is doing at that moment. Quite rattled, Claire continues giving her update and stays on the call until the end. By that time Jacob has left. She now ponders what she should do: ignore the situation or confront Jacob and tell him his behavior was disturbing during this important call with the client. She also stops to consider if Jacob's behavior is the only problem she has to address.

Effective Conversations

The purpose of an effective conversation is to develop a free flow of relevant information. You do this through dialogue where people are openly and honestly expressing their opinions, sharing their feelings, and articulating their theories willingly, even when their ideas are controversial or unpopular.[2]

Dialogue is a two-way exchange of information and ideas. For a conversation to be effective, all the individuals involved have to enter it with open minds, be present in the moment, and be aware of what's happening and what's being said. It also helps if both people can approach the conversation in a non-judgmental manner. You can encourage dialogue by:

* ✳ Being at ease—it will put the others at ease.

* ✳ Getting the other person's perspective. Asking others to contribute and provide opinions is a compliment.

* ✳ Showing sensitivity and listening for statements that may lead to new or additional information.

* ✳ Checking for understanding by repeating, paraphrasing, and taking time to reflect before stating your immediate reaction. Don't assume that everybody sees things the same as you.

* ✳ Using listening skills. Being patient.[3]

➥ Chapter 5: Listen Up!

There are a variety of skills that can help you and others engage in meaningful dialogue.

Attending skills are very helpful in establishing ease. Sit next to each other, rather than across the table or room. It puts everyone on an even level. Maintaining good eye contact and using appropriate gestures and a warm tone of voice convey that you are attending to and in tune with each other. Using phases such as "I see," "I hear you," and "I understand" also convey that you are acknowledging what is being said. Keep in mind that such acknowledgment by the other person doesn't necessarily signal that they are in agreement with you. Acknowledgment is recognition; it is the essential element of respect.

Encouraging skills should be used when you have a need for the other person to elaborate on his/her thoughts or feelings. Encouraging skills use statements and questions such as:

* ❋ I'd like to know how you feel about it.
* ❋ Would you like to talk about it? Tell me more about it.
* ❋ Is there anything else you'd like to say?
* ❋ Perhaps you could tell me about....
* ❋ Is there anything else I should know?

Clarifying skills should be used when you are unsure what the other person is saying and you want to reduce ambiguity and establish clarity. Clarifying skills use statements and questions such as:

* ❋ What I think you are saying is...
* ❋ Could you give me an example of...?
* ❋ I'm not sure I understand. Could you repeat that?
* ❋ Could you tell me more about...?

Different words have different meanings to different people. Be sure to explain terms and jargon so others know what you mean. Don't assume that other people will know what you mean.

Reflecting skills allow you to restate, in your own words, what the other person is saying. You can reflect on either the content or the feeling that is being expressed. It shows understanding and acceptance and allows you to keep the conversation on track. Reflecting skills use statements such as:

✳ It sounds as if you really...

✳ Do you think it's a good idea if...?

✳ You would really like it if...

✳ You think that...[4]

What discourages dialogue in organizations? Some people are conflict averse. For them, it's easier to be silent. Some organizations or professions are hierarchical in nature and confronting situations and problems is not part of their culture. Some people want to defer to authority (especially when that's the culture of the organization) even if they have information or experience that is contrary to their manager's or other senior leader's position. Staff members don't want to run the risk of upsetting the boss. Sometimes situations are just plain embarrassing or personal such as hygiene or dress code issues. Failing to confront a difficult situation doesn't solve anything. Issues go underground and problems fester. People get discouraged and leave, taking their institutional knowledge and talent with them. Managers don't receive either meaningful feedback or crucial information. Mistakes are made and nobody wins, especially the organization.

Louise is one of the most efficient and effective employees Harrison ever hired. There's no task she won't do when asked. As the receptionist, she's great on the phone and with greeting visitors to the office. She'd be the perfect employee, except for the tight, low-cut tops she wears that show too much cleavage.

Recognizing that this is going to be a difficult conversation to have with her, Harrison ponders his options: avoid the situation because no one has complained, ask a female colleague to talk to her, or prepare for her reaction and talk to her himself.

Get Good Information

For a conversation to be free flowing, everyone involved has to be prepared to get and to give information in a constructive, collaborative manner. Each person comes into the conversation with his/her own opinions, feelings, beliefs, theories, histories, and experiences. The objective is to create an environment or pool where people can collectively share their ideas and information so the pool becomes rich and deep with information. The deeper the pool, the more trusting the environment, the better positioned the parties are to make the best possible decisions.[5] As you work to create a two-way exchange of information, stay flexible about who asks the questions and who states concerns or provides information first.

In order to obtain good information, you have to learn to ask a number of different types of questions and practice different questioning techniques. Each serves a specific purpose and should be used appropriately and interchangeably.

* **Open-ended questions** provide an opportunity for the other person to tell it in his/her own words. They often give the greatest amount of information.

Examples: "Tell me what happened." "Help me better understand." "Can you say a little more about how you see things?" "Tell me why this is important."

❋ **Closed-ended questions** provide limited answers. They are useful to obtain specific information or to clarify facts. You may need to use them to keep the discussion focused and on track.

Examples: "Did you tell Jean you would be late for work?" "Did you fail to send the e-mail as you were instructed?"

❋ **Reflective questions** provide an opportunity to clarify information previously stated. They are helpful if information appears to be conflicting, or if the other person appears to be uncertain or hesitant.

Examples: "Did you say that you called in sick on Monday or Tuesday?" "Do I understand that you never received the document you were asked to review?"

❋ **Factual questions** provide specific and targeted information. They are helpful in separating facts from assumptions. You may want to use them when you need to ask for supporting facts, documents, or other evidence. You can verify the answers to factual questions by checking a second or third source.

Examples: "How many people overheard the conversation?" "On what date did you receive that phone call?"

✳ **Opinion-based questions** provide the other person with an opportunity to clarify his/her beliefs, attitudes, and opinions. They are useful in distinguishing first- from second-hand knowledge.

Examples: "What do you mean she has a poor attitude?" "Do you think that your manager treats men more favorably than women?"

✳ **Descriptive questions** provide an opportunity to describe the events or give a narrative account.

Examples: "Describe the events leading up to your manager screaming at the staff." "Tell me exactly what happened on Monday afternoon."

✳ **Feeling or emotive questions** provide the other person the opportunity to describe his/her feelings.

Examples: "How did you feel when she said that to you?" "What was your reaction to his statement?"

Be curious and probe. Ask who, what, when, where, and why questions and clarify terminology and acronyms. It is also important to ask for concrete or relevant information. For example:

✳ "What leads you to say that?"

✳ "Can you give me an example?"

✳ "How would that work?"

It is equally important for the conversation and thought process to flow. Too many questions and interjections could disrupt this flow. Though you need to control the time and the discussion, don't control the direction of the discussion. Talking too much may be a barrier that contributes to the erosion of communication.

Push other people to be specific, using the following probes:

* ✳ "Please fill me in on the details."
* ✳ "Can you give me a specific example of what happened?"
* ✳ "Do you have a particular situation in mind?"
* ✳ "What exactly do you want me to do?"[6]

Give Good Information

When you give information, you want it to be relevant, precise, and accurate. You want to assure that the other person receives the information you intend for them to have. Beware of providing too much information at one time because it could be overwhelming.

Be specific and provide details. Ask yourself, "What information do I have that the other person needs?" Lack of specificity causes problems. Tasks go uncompleted and questions fail to get answered because people are not mind readers. Be honest and positive rather than negative. We hear and remember positive words better than negative words and the listener is more likely to remember what you said. Be accurate and check your facts.[7]

You want to get and give good information in order to get to the root cause of the problem. During your discussion, be sure that you:

* ✳ Explain the problem as you see it without judgment.

* Ask the other person to explain the problem from his/her point of view.

* Ask for clarity.

* Keep the person and attitudes separate from this issue.

* Are factual.

* Describe behavior you observe.

* Avoid subjective language.

Beyond the Facts—Feelings

Understand that feelings are normal and natural. Without them we wouldn't be human. Learn to recognize and acknowledge them. They are part of who you are—your emotional intelligence. Your awareness of and your ability to express your feelings and emotions will vary depending on the relationship you're in at any given time. Recognizing this helps you to understand what you're feeling and why. Just as you have feelings, so do the other parties to your conflict and conversations. Their feelings are important, and so are yours.[8]

In order to keep the conversation positive and productive, learn to listen for emotions and attitudes. Is the other person expressing his/her feelings either directly or indirectly? What feelings is he displaying and is he aware of his feelings? How are they impacting the conversation and the situation?

Victor and Raymond are involved in a conversation about their respective roles and responsibilities. Raymond starts to take the conversation off course by bringing up unrelated issues in a cool, somewhat calculating manner. Victor

can feel himself getting angry—he's even starting to sweat—but he doesn't want to lose his
temper. He raises his hand to indicate a halt
and says, "I think we need to take a break and
resume this later."

Don't try to control the other person's reactions or
emotions. Instead, prepare for it. If you're initiating the
conversation, think of how it might go. Put yourself in
the other person's place. Think about how their reactions might affect you and throw you off balance. The
more prepared you are, the less likely it is that you'll be
blindsided.

Remember: The goal of the conversation is to keep
the facts central to the issue while at the same time
acknowledging that people and their emotions are
often integral parts of the interaction. To do this, you
need to maintain balance and control. In an emotion-
ally charged situation, it might be easy to assume that
feelings are irrelevant and wouldn't be helpful to share.
Try restating your assumption by acknowledging that
feelings are at the heart of the situation and are complex, and acknowledge that you have to explore further
to understand your own feelings. This moves you from
avoidance of your feelings to addressing them (yours
and theirs) in a non-judgmental manner. Acknowledge
feelings before you embark on problem solving.[9]

Maintain control and balance if feelings and emotions begin to dominate the conversation. Doing so
will build constructive relationships, maintain the
confidence and self-esteem of all the parties involved,
and ensure that there is integrity in the process and
the relationships. Here are some tips for doing so:

❋ Maintain a level-headed response to others' intense emotions and don't let them push your buttons.

❋ Don't absorb their issues or unrealistic expectations; give them a shot of reality.

❋ Stick to the facts and the issues.

❋ Remain objective and neutral.

❋ Be understanding. The other person may be deflecting his or her emotions toward you.

❋ Acknowledge the behavior in a calm manner.

❋ Model constructive behavior.

❋ Use a soft approach by softening your voice, posture, tone, eye contact, and body language; it sends a message of openness.

❋ Breathe deeply and don't become defensive.

❋ Avoid sounding patronizing, even if you are frustrated.

❋ Avoid interrupting, unless it's to get a conversation back on track.

❋ Use tact and sensitivity.

❋ Propose an approach to refocus.

❋ Determine if you can continue in a constructive way at this time.

➥ Appendix: Working With Emotions

A Second Look

What could the owner at the local eatery have done differently to solve the problem that was central to this conflict? Rather than look back and assign blame, she could have looked forward and begun to understand the problem. When she placed blame, she made a bad judgment call that hindered her ability to understand and solve the problem.

She should have looked at the receipt that the customer sent, which detailed the order. She should have questioned the manager who was on duty that morning to confirm what the breakfast special was and compared it to the order. She should have inquired who was working the counter and who was working in the kitchen. She failed to question whether or not procedures had been followed. The problem may have been with the motivation and/or ability of one of the staff members—either someone who worked in the kitchen or someone who worked the counter. She failed to look at the systems in the establishment as a whole to see if there was room for process improvement. Without getting some simple facts, she hindered her ability to get to the root cause of the problem and address it.

Claire's dilemma is different. There is more than one issue here, and potentially several. The first is that Jacob's behavior—barging into her office and breathing down her neck during an important call with the client—was unexpected and unnerving for her. The second issue is that Jacob is new to both the organization and the industry, and appears to be unaware of its culture.

Because this is the first time Claire has encountered this behavior by Jacob, she decides to confront it now while the situation is still fresh and recent. In preparing to speak to him, she clarifies the issue she needs to confront and asks herself what the consequences are to her, to her relationship with Jacob, to her relationship with the client, and to the project.[10] This allows her to focus, to explain the impact his behavior had on her, and to provide him with information about the client and the project. It will also give her an opportunity to talk about expectations—what she expects from him and what he expects from her.

➡ Chapter 6: You Want Me to Do What?

As appealing as the other two options are, Harrison knows that he has to have a talk with Louise. He knows avoiding the problem will not make it go away, and in the long run will grow worse and may even be costly. It could just take one snide remark about her appearance for a harassment claim to surface.

As uncomfortable as the situation may be for him, shirking his responsibility and asking a female colleague or human resources to handle his employee issue could ruin his relationship with Louise. She may no longer respect him (or his authority) as her manager. The only way to address this issue is to prepare for a possibly negative reaction and confront Louise. Of course, he may seek help and guidance in the way of role-playing from a colleague or human resources as part of his preparation.

➡ Chapter 9: Whose Fight Is It Anyway?

Victor left the building after his confrontation with Raymond. To cool off, he took a walk around the office park where his company's offices were located. By taking this time out and leaving an emotional situation, he was able to reflect. He is keenly aware of his tendency to become angry and sometimes act out on that anger. He could feel his body reacting. He didn't want to get knocked off balance. With his head clear, he can return to his office and prepare how he will resume the conversation with Raymond.

Essential Tips

* ✢ Have dialogues, not monologues.
* ✢ Ask questions that will get you the facts and information that you need.
* ✢ Remain factual and provide information in a non-judgmental manner.
* ✢ Don't try to control someone else's reactions and emotions—prepare for them.
* ✢ Keep an open mind and remain unbiased.
* ✢ Use good judgment.
* ✢ Don't make assumptions.

CHAPTER 5
LISTEN UP!

If the person you're talking to isn't listening, be patient. Maybe he has a small piece of fluff in his ear.

—Winnie-the-Pooh

Listening is probably the most misunderstood communication process we use. Listening is not waiting for your turn to talk, but it appears that is how most of us listen—while the other person is talking, all we're doing is thinking about what we are going to say next—and, because we aren't *hearing* what is being said, the odds are our response doesn't move the communication process forward.

"Listening well is essential for workplace success. The U.S. Department of Labor estimates that of the total time we spend in communication, 22 percent is devoted to reading and writing, 23 percent to speaking—and 55 percent to listening."[1]

Jenny and Bob are working together on a team project that requires them to make a presentation to their company's leadership team next week. Jenny says, "Bob, we need to get this finished today in order to have time to practice so we can be perfect by next week. Can you spare some time today to work with me on the final slides?"

While she's speaking, Bob hears Jenny say they're going to have to work late tonight and he has to be at his son's school event. He interrupts her to say, "I can't, Jenny. I have to leave on time today to get to Colin's play. You'll have to finish it on your own."

Jenny is totally confused and says, "How come I have to do all the work? You're always letting me and the team down."

Bob gets mad at her accusation that he isn't a team player and storms out of her office. Jenny stares at his back as he leaves the room and wonders what just happened!

Listening is hard work, and most of the time when we think of communication, we focus on words—either in writing or speaking—and we don't spend a lot of time learning how to listen. In her book, *The Power of a Good Fight*, Lynne Eisaguirre says:

Part of the problem is our lack of understanding about how our minds work and how the mind and our senses interact, especially what we hold in our minds as "truths." Our hearing is ever present. There is no switch to turn it off. We can close our eyes, but not our ears. We live in a culture where we're constantly bombarded by sounds; our sense of balance is tied to our hearing. It's no accident that so many of us feel constantly out of balance because of the bombardment of information from inside our minds as well as external sounds.[2]

There are many things that get in the way as we listen or even try to listen. Consider, for example:

❋ Setting—what else is going on when you are having a conversation? Are you in a private setting where it is quiet and, therefore, easy to hear what is being said? Or, are you trying to have a substantive discussion in a noisy restaurant or any place where there are a lot of distractions?

❋ Timing—are both people in the conversation ready to talk about a particular subject at this time? Consider how difficult it is to listen when the other person has brought up a subject you weren't expecting and you need time to think about how you really want to proceed.

❋ Beliefs—what beliefs do I hold that are potentially in conflict with the person with whom I am communicating?

✳ Perceptions—what preconceived ideas do I have about the person across from me? Am I reacting to how he/she is dressed or how he/she speaks?

✳ Emotions—am I having a bad day? Did I come to work today with emotional baggage left from something that happened at home this morning?

✳ Cultural differences—is this person from a different part of the world or a different religion?

✳ Relationships—do I compete with this person for "face time" with the CEO? Do we have a natural rivalry? Might this person stand in my way for a promotion?

✳ Words—does this person use words I don't understand?

✳ Assumptions—am I applying my own assumptions to what the speaker is saying?

➥ Chapter 2: Why Can't Everyone Be Like Me?

Jennifer Nycz-Connor writes, "Don't make the classic mistake of assuming when you should be listening. As managers, we miss cues when employees are frustrated or unhappy, and it's only when they hand us their resignations that our hindsight kicks in. Take some time to actively listen to those around you."[3]

When there's conflict, it is extremely important for the parties to come together in person rather than trying to resolve their differences by phone or, perish the thought, by e-mail or text messages. Why? Because we communicate with more than just words. Many times non-verbal cues that are impossible to see or feel unless you are face to face, make or break the discussion. E-communications are primarily a text medium with no social interaction. They don't convey body language, expressions, tone or voice, and other subtleties that exist in face-to-face communication. E-communications are composed and not spontaneous and, there is no immediate feedback or acknowledgment and no guarantee that a message is heard. And, when the stakes are high and resolving the issue is critical personally or professionally, communicating in person takes on even more importance! However, when you work remotely or in different cities, states, or countries, face-to-face communication may be impossible, so pick up the phone and have a two-way conversation.

➡ Chapter 4: What's the Problem?

Mike and Lynne work in two different departments for a small organization. Their offices are about 50 feet apart. They both are very passionate about their work, but neither is very patient. They each will fight to the end for their point of view which, more often than not, does not agree with the other's position on the issue at hand. So, consider this e-mail exchange:

Mike sends Lynne the first e-mail to say that one of his employees had trouble logging on to the time and attendance software three times this week and Lynne's help desk wasn't helpful. He says to her, "Fix it!"

Lynne responds immediately with a terse message that says, "Your employee must not know how to use the system. It works for everyone else." Mike responds in an equally hostile manner and the chain of e-mails goes on 19 times. Remember: These are people who work in the same office, 50 feet away from each other! This conflict will never be resolved unless they get together, *listen* to each other, and observe the non-verbal cues.

What does it feel like when you know that someone is really listening to what you are saying? The odds are that it feels pretty good and, unfortunately, we don't get that feeling often enough. When you are listened to, you feel satisfied, respected, and that what you're saying was heard. What we really want is to be heard and understood.

This is especially true when applying good listening techniques to resolving (or even preventing) conflict in the workplace. Listening is a powerful part of the communication process that can help any of us increase our effectiveness—and not just at work. Think about how it feels in your personal life when a spouse, child, parent, sibling, or friend really gets what you are trying to say—when they hear you!

Listening takes place in three stages: receiving, processing, and responding. In *the receiving* phase, if you are the listener, you have to take in or receive what the other person is saying. You need to carefully listen to the words, observe body language if you are speaking face to face, and, if you are a really good listener with well-honed skills, you will listen for what is not being said as well. Some people call this "listening for the music—not just the words," or as Shannon L. Adler said, "The most important thing in communication is hearing what isn't being said. The art of reading between the lines is a lifelong quest of the wise."[4]

As the speaker is talking, you as the listener begin *to process* what your ears and eyes are taking in. Your mind starts to process the information you've heard. You try to understand what you've heard so that you know what it is they are asking or telling you. This is a very private process and takes place in your brain in a very short period of time. This process has to take place so that you as the listener can respond to the speaker.

Then, you *respond* to what you've heard and what your brain has processed. If you've listened carefully and observed all the visual cues available to you, hopefully you've understood what the speaker intended and you respond in a way that lets the speaker know he/she was heard. This then allows the two of you to move forward in a highly productive way. If you've misunderstood something that was said, or the intent, then the speaker has an opportunity to correct your assumption, hopefully in a manner that illuminates the issue. The connection has then been made.

➥ Appendix: The Communication Cycle

Sam and Ralph have worked together for many years and have a very positive working relationship. One day, Sam goes to Ralph's office to discuss an idea he's come up with that will have a big impact on Ralph's department. Sam says, "I've come up with something that your department needs to do right away!"

Ralph puts up a hand to stop him talking and yells, "Who are you to tell me what to do?"

Sam quickly responds, "I guess I didn't say that right."

Because the world we live and work in moves so quickly, it's critical to try to slow down when listening in a conflict management situation so as not to create misunderstandings. We've all gotten good at ignoring some things we hear while focusing on other things being said. In other words, we jump to conclusions. Sometimes, we jump to the right conclusion, but sometimes we totally miss the mark and make matters worse. Because we move so quickly from what we hear to forming a conclusion, we may not be aware that we've missed out on some valuable information along the way. Remember the restaurant owner in Chapter 4 who was too quick to jump to the wrong conclusion?

To avoid jumping to conclusions, you may want to take the time to have each person describe what they heard before moving on to trying to resolve the conflict.

Carol hears from a coworker that the entire team is going to have to work this coming weekend. Before she clarifies the message, she rushes into her manager's office, interrupts her phone call, and yells that this is unacceptable—they should have discussed this at the staff meeting yesterday and, besides, she can't work on the weekend because it is her wedding anniversary and they are going away. Her boss quickly stands up and says, "Carol, you're really out of line here and don't speak to me in that tone."

When they cool down, the manager lets Carol know that she wasn't on the list for the weekend project; she'd gotten bad information.

Active Listening

Active listening is the most powerful way to capture the entire message the speaker is attempting to convey. Active listening encourages the other person to talk. As an active listener, you capture both the words and the music. And the speaker gets the message that you really *heard* what he/she was saying and the actual message he/she wanted to share with you. Active listening takes some work and some practice, but the payoff is high. Active listening is critical to resolving conflict in the workplace, so it is worth taking the time to learn and practice the techniques. Active listening, however, is not about agreeing with everything the other person is saying; it is about achieving in a non-judgmental way an understanding of what the person speaking means.

Here's how it works:

While the speaker is talking, the active listener sends messages to encourage the speaker to provide more information or to show more emotion. This is done in several ways, including a smile, a nod, a raised eyebrow, but especially by having the listener maintain eye contact with the speaker. In order for active listening to work, the listener has to sincerely want to hear what is being said. Consider how it would feel if you were sharing an extremely serious subject with a colleague who, while you're pouring your heart out, is rolling his/her eyes or smiling? You'd probably stop talking and walk away, and the communication cycle would be broken.

On the flip side, if while you are talking the listener nods to indicate he/she understands how important this topic is to you, chances are you'd want to continue the conversation and maybe, just maybe, you'd share even more information than you originally intended.

However, as the listener, non-verbal communication isn't enough in the active listening process. You'll need to get comfortable with some quick and easy words or phrases to let the speaker know you are really paying attention.

Consider words and phrases such as:

* Yes.
* I see.
* Really?
* Great.
* Oh.
* That's interesting.

How you say the previous words and phrases is also important. Your tone has to be non-judgmental and especially not flippant or sarcastic. Remember: Your intent here is to learn as much as you can about what the speaker is saying, so be encouraging.

Another way to move the process forward is to repeat what the speaker has said—a word or a phrase that you want to know more about or to understand better. To do this you need to repeat exactly what the speaker said and make it a question so that the speaker then amplifies what they meant. This is especially helpful if the speaker says something that is less than specific or uses a word or phrase that you don't understand.

As you are learning the active listening technique, remember the idea that asking open-ended questions gets you a lot more information than closed-ended questions. For example:

Ask "What did you think were the main points of the report?" rather than "Did you like the report?"

Ask "How do you think we could get the information we need to make a good decision?" rather than "Do you have everything you need to decide?"

Use probes to get additional information, such as, "Tell me more," "How so?" "Why?" and, if you're good with it, use silence. Most people are uncomfortable with periods of silence and will fill it up with information. It may be just the information you need and you might not have gotten it any other way than by being silent.

Another effective active listening technique is to paraphrase what you've heard the speaker saying. Try to do it in one sentence by saying, "What I heard you say was..." or "It sounds like what I heard you say was...."

➡ Chapter 4: What's the Problem?

Carrie and Maggie have worked together for years, but sometimes find themselves at odds on how to manage the work in their department. One day, Maggie says to Carrie, "In the staff meeting yesterday, you came across as too critical of the IT department and the work they did on the roll-out of our company intranet."

The good news is both of them had just participated in a webinar on active listening, so Carrie took the opportunity to put into practice what she'd learned.

While Maggie was speaking, Carrie watched for non-verbal cues and saw that Maggie's body language indicated she wasn't angry about the meeting. She noticed Maggie smiled when she made her statements that could have been a criticism of Carrie but, in reality, were words she could take in a positive manner and learn from them. Before she responded, she paused for a moment to think about what she'd just heard, which was difficult for her because she'd always been someone who was quick to speak and usually had her response prepared before the other person stopped speaking. She asked for clarification.

"Thanks for letting me know. Can you tell me more about what you heard me say and why you thought it could be interpreted as criticism?" This exchange, using active listening techniques, proved to be successful in moving the dialogue forward in a positive manner.

Active Listening means making a deliberate effort to understand what the other person's message is from his/her point of view, paying attention to all verbal and non-verbal signals, clarifying meaning when you don't understand, and rephrasing and showing your desire to understand what is being said.

* Listen to learn. Be interested and show it.
* Seek understanding. Listen to words and clarify understanding.

✳ Turn off your listening filters. Don't allow yourself to think of anything except what the speaker is saying.

✳ Be patient. Avoid interrupting the person during his/her explanation.

✳ Withhold judgment until you have all the facts.

✳ Focus on content as well as delivery.

✳ Pay attention to non-verbal signals.

✳ Recognize that listening is not waiting for your turn to talk. The absence of talk is not the same as listening. Pausing during your discussion may prompt the person to volunteer additional relevant information.

✳ Resist the urge to formulate a response until after the speaker is finished.

✳ Listen with compassion. Be aware of your tone of voice and body language.

✳ Listen for feelings as well as facts.

✳ Listen for what is not said, and use the opportunity to probe for more information.

✳ Listen for what you don't want to hear as well as what you do want to hear.

✳ Listen long enough to understand what the other person is telling you.[5]

Reflective Listening

When you're listening carefully and watching for non-verbal cues, you are acting like a mirror to reflect back emotions you sense. These emotions, most likely, carry a great deal of the message the speaker is attempting to convey. You can reflect on either the content or the feeling that is being expressed. It shows understanding and acceptance and allows you to keep the conversation on track. It's important to put the comment/probe in the form of a question in order to get the speaker to confirm, deny, or clarify what was said. Keep your questions and your tone pitched at a low level so that the speaker doesn't feel attacked. To encourage reflective listening, consider comments and questions such as:

* "It sounds like that was a fun experience. Did I hear you correctly?"

* "Wow. That must have hurt. Are you okay?"

* "I'm hearing frustration in your voice. Is that so?"

* "It sounds as if you really...."

* "Do you think it's a good idea if...?"

* "You would really like it if...."

* "Do you think that...?"

➡ Appendix: Self-Reflection Exercise—
What Is Your Listening Style?

One way to resolve conflict in the workplace is to have a productive dialogue where both people in the situation are able to get their points across. Here are some ways to encourage dialogue:

* Put the other person at ease and start with some small talk.

* Sit next to each other rather than across from each other.

* Maintain good eye contact.

❊ Use appropriate gestures.

❊ Speak in a warm, welcoming tone of voice.

❊ Use phrases such as "I see," "I hear you," and "I understand."

❊ Be sensitive to the other person's frame of mind.

❊ Be patient and don't interrupt the other speaker until he/she is finished talking.

❊ Use the active or reflective listening skills described previously.

Listening Filters

As Mark Goulston writes, "...without realizing it, we categorize people instantly in the following sequence:

❊ Gender.

❊ Generation (age).

❊ Nationality (or ethnicity).

❊ Education level.

❊ Emotion.

The sequence goes in this order because we see a person's gender, generation, and nationality first, hear the person's educational level second, and feel the person's level of emotionality third. Keep (this) in mind, and it'll help you to spot subconscious filters that keep you from listening to—and reaching—other people."[6]

➡ Appendix: Barriers to Communication

> Listening isn't easy, but good listening skills can be learned and practiced at work and at home. You know how it feels when you are communicating with someone and you know he/she is sincerely interested in not just hearing you, but understanding why this is important to you and what his/her role is in making whatever needs to be done happen.

If you are in a conflict situation and you want to know where the other person is coming from and you really want to resolve the conflict, then follow these tips:

❊ Be sincere.

❊ Be curious.

❊ Be understanding.

❊ Be patient.

Listening well helps us manage conflict. It's not easy to slow down and take the time to really hear what the other person is saying. Or as Lynne Eisaguirre puts it in *The Power of a Good Fight*, "We can be passionate about our listening. We can learn to listen with as much energy and enthusiasm as we talk. Instead of listening for evidence that confirms our point of view, we can listen for the creative energy in the conflict—both in ourselves and in others."[7]

Answer the Question That Was Asked!

Here's a real conversation that shows the importance of answering the question that is asked.

Adam: "We haven't heard from Tony since he returned from his vacation cruise."

Gracie: "How long was he away?"

Adam: "He got back about two weeks ago—about the 29th."

Gracie: "That's not what I asked. I asked how long he'd been gone—not when he got back—because I had no idea he was even away!"

As John Marshall, Chief Justice of the Supreme Court said, "To listen well is as powerful a means of communication and influence as to talk well."[8]

Essential Tips

* ✶ Listening takes work, but the payoff is great.

* ✶ Listening isn't about planning what you're going to say while the other person is still speaking.

* ✶ Consider what gets in the way of you being a good listener: the setting, timing, your beliefs, your emotions, any cultural differences, your relationship with the speaker, or the words being used.

* ✶ There are three stages of listening: receiving, processing, and responding.

* Active listening allows the listener both the words and the music.

* When you use reflective listening, you're acting like a mirror to reflect back what emotions you hear.

* Good listening habits help to manage conflict.

CHAPTER 6

YOU WANT ME TO DO WHAT?

If I want to know how I'm doing at work, I don't wait for a pat on the back. I ask the people who will give me a clear, objective opinion.

—Chandra Wilson

Looking back, it was a great first day of work for Violet. Just re-entering the workforce after a break to raise her children, the job was not very demanding, but there was potential for more opportunity. During the interview, her manager, Enrique, clearly explained what the job entailed—its functions and the tasks she would be expected to perform—and how the job related to others in the department. On her first day, he reinforced everything they'd discussed in the interview about her job and the department, its values of integrity and respect, and its commitment to service for the organization's patrons. Coming out of a staff meeting six months later, Violet reflected on how much she admired Enrique as a manager. He lets you know what he expects and you always know where you stand with him. He also models the values of the department.

Communicate Early and Often

At the core of many workplace conflicts is the lack of clear expectations. If people don't understand what the organization, their manager, or their teammates and peers expect, the results can be confusion and conflict. There is a golden opportunity to set the tone early, beginning with the interview, just as Enrique did. He set expectations for the role and what success in the role looks like. The next opportunity is at the beginning of the employment relationship—especially during the on-boarding or orientation process—when the organization's culture should be introduced. Let employees know: "These are our values, these are the behaviors that reflect our values, and we have zero tolerance for behavior that is contrary to our values, such as harassment, discrimination, workplace bullying, etc. Any type of disrespectful behavior has no place in our workplace."

➡ Chapter 11: What's an Organization to Do?

Enrique continues to reinforce expectations and values both in staff meetings and in individual meetings with his employees. During today's staff meeting, he emphasized the importance of communicating patrons' issues to management using Rita's recent situation. Rita, who serves as a guide, noticed that a blind patron had a preference for using the stairs rather than the elevators which is marked in Braille. As a guide, Rita knows that she has to respect the patrons' wishes and not try to persuade them to take another course, in this case the elevator. However, she let Enrique know so he could take action to get the stairs marked in Braille as well. The blind patrons were served with dignity and respect! Enrique took this opportunity to give accolades to Rita for the way she handled the situation.

Clear expectations establish an understanding about:

✳ What an employee's job entails, such as its functions and tasks.

✳ How the job supports the goals and values of the organization.

✳ Why the job is important and how it supports other jobs in the organization.

✳ What good job performance means: successful outputs and results.

✳ The impact of good performance on others, the organization, and its stakeholders.

Remember that words can have different meanings. Be sure to:

✳ Speak clearly.

✳ Define terms.

❋ Avoid jargon.

❋ Check for understanding.

Expectations Equal Accountability

Last month's staff meeting was a different story, however. Because she was new, Violet didn't have any past experience with it, but there'd been a change in how the paid time off policy would be applied and it had a negative impact on most of the part-time staff in the department. To his credit, Violet thought, Enrique explained the problem in a very straightforward and factual manner. He explained the policy and how he had allowed it to be misapplied. He apologized for his role in the misinterpretation of the policy and acknowledged the negative impact it would have on the staff. He was empathic toward the staff, yet clear that going forward the policy would be applied as it was intended. He explained that the policy set certain standards to which everyone was expected to adhere. He recognized that there had been an oversight on his part in the past and was accountable for his error. He took responsibility. During lunch after the meeting, some of her coworkers were complaining about the policy and Enrique. Violet took the opportunity to tell them about her friend Angelia.

Angelia has been working at her current job for two years. She recently completed a report using the criteria and standard format that had been established. Her boss called her out on it, telling her that what he wanted wasn't in the report. When she asked what was missing or wrong, he told her she should know and provided no further direction or details. This had happened in the past to both Angelia and another coworker. The next day in a staff meeting, the boss advised in very general terms that reports needed to be completed correctly. He provided no specific details or examples. Angelia is frustrated. The established standards were not being honored, she received no specific details on how her report could have been improved, and her boss chose to provide a vague description of expectations that no one on the staff understood! Enrique, Violet pointed out, lives up to the expectations that he sets for everyone—integrity and respect. On the other hand, Angelia's boss doesn't even honor the standards that have been set for certain tasks within the department.

Leo is a supervisor in a pharmaceutical manufacturing company. Derrick failed to follow a quality process. When Leo quietly points it out, Derrick becomes defensive. Leo responds immediately by calling a relief worker to take over, and brings Derrick into his private office, where he quietly reviews the process, explaining why it exists, and the consequences for not following it. The process is a fair procedure—an objective criterion—based on standards drawn from scientific judgment and the common interest of the community. The process and standards are reviewed early and often in the employment relationship, and employees are expected to adhere to them. Leo holds himself and his department accountable to those standards, unlike Angelia's boss who often disregards the standards.

➡ Chapter 7: Don't Draw a Line in the Sand!

Consider another situation where an employee, Chris, made a commitment to attend an important meeting and missed it. His boss thinks he missed it on purpose. He calls Chris aside privately and, like Leo, describes what was expected and what was observed.

"Chris, I noticed that you missed the meeting you agreed to attend. What happened? Did you run into a problem of some kind?"[1] Commitments are a type of expectation, agreements that individuals make to each other. When commitments are broken and account-ability is not taken, conflicts arise. Chris's boss pointed out the broken commitment in a non-confrontational manner, similar to Leo's approach.

Motivation or Ability?

If expectations aren't being met, is it because the individual(s) can't or won't meet them? In other words, is it a problem with motivation or ability or possibly both? If the individual *could* perform as expected, in fact has performed in the past, but does not do so now, he may lack the desire or motivation to perform according to expectations. On the other hand, if the individual *wants to* perform as expected, but fails to do so, then she may lack the knowledge or skill to perform according to standards.

If motivation is at the root of the issue, the challenge becomes changing behavior. Pointing out the consequences of the behavior is a critical step. If the individual understands the consequences, changes to his or her behavior will likely follow.

> If motivation is the problem, consider the following questions:
>
> ✳   How do you go about motivating others to change their behavior?

> ✳ How do you get people to understand that
> their existing view of the consequences is ei-
> ther inaccurate or incomplete?[2]

One of Leo's colleagues, Bruce, is having a difficult time with his assistant, Leah. She is constantly making mistakes, especially when it comes to updating his appointments. When he sits down to talk with her, Bruce explains that her errors are causing more work for the other assistants. "I'm sure it's a hassle to double-check appointments when you enter them, but our current error rate is so high that the assistants in the other departments are calling me to ask for confirmation. I worry if your reputation here is going to be hurt if we can't solve this."[3]

Bruce takes it one step further. He ties his expectations of Leah's work to the company's values. As a pharmaceutical company, quality is highly valued, not only in the manufacturing process, but throughout the organization. Bruce reviews the expectations of quality for the administrative staff that Leah is not meeting:

✳ The ability to produce work products accurately and free of errors.

✳ The ability to recognize and correct errors.

✳ The ability to proofread and check your work and be attentive to detail.

Bruce did two very important things in this conversation. He explained the consequences of Leah's behavior and its impact on others, and he reviewed his expectations, which were based on company standards and values. Behavioral expectations provide a means for objective evaluation that minimizes bias and provides meaningful information.[4]

Expectations based on performance standards are powerful in diffusing an argument and stopping a conflict in its tracks. June described a situation with an applicant who had taken and failed a data entry test several times because her error rate exceeded the standard. English was not the applicant's first language, and she had difficulty understanding why she wasn't hired. Her irate husband called in screaming at June, threatening to go over her head and call the company's president. June waited for the chance to responds then calmly explained the criteria against which his wife's performance was measured. After a long pause, he apologized; he now understood. June neutralized his behavior and its impact. Rather than react, she took away his stick—his perceived power and desire to go over her head to the president—by providing the facts.[5]

If it's ability, rather than motivation, the challenge becomes improving performance through training or coaching. Consider Yusuf's dilemma. He's new to the organization and quickly realizes that Shelton is an average-to-poor writer. When he sits down to talk with him, Shelton becomes very defensive stating that he never received negative feedback about his writing skills from his former manager, Warren. He shuts down, refusing to acknowledge or respond to any of Yusuf's further comments. During lunch, Shelton vents to his colleague about how unfair Yusuf is being. After all, their former manager was always satisfied with his work. His colleague confides that Warren often rewrote some of Shelton's work because Warren was a non-confrontational type. He tells Shelton he agrees with Yusuf that Shelton's writing is mediocre.

Yusuf, in the meantime, realizes that he has inherited a problem that was probably never addressed in the past. Although Shelton's writing is barely acceptable, it's not beyond help. There is still an opportunity for improvement. He asks himself a number of questions, including:

✳ What are the specific facts of this performance issue?

✳ Am I approaching this situation with the goal of creating an opportunity for this employee to be successful in the future?[6]

Realizing that Shelton has been operating under the illusion of competency for quite some time, Yusuf needs to create an opportunity for Shelton. He calls HR for advice and information about the company's educational assistance program and individual development and improvement processes.

The next time they meet, Yusuf thanks Shelton for coming to this meeting with an open mind and acknowledges that Shelton was probably caught off guard by his feedback at the last meeting. He emphasizes that his expectations are different from Warren's and reviews his expectations with Shelton. He provides examples of Shelton's writing that don't meet these expectations. Finally, he suggests that they work on a plan together to help Shelton strengthen his skills and improve his performance. After some discussion, they agree on the following:

✳ Shelton will allow more time for planning and revising his writing assignments.

✳ Yusuf or a designated colleague will review Shelton's drafts and provide constructive feedback.

✳ A writing coach will be identified to work with Shelton and the company will pay the cost.

✳   Shelton will work with the coach on his own time for a 90-day period.

> Here are some hallmarks of effective performance appraisals:
>
> ✳ Active employee participation.
>
> ✳ A positive attitude.
>
> ✳ Mutual problem solving.
>
> ✳ Mutual goal setting.
>
> ✳ Clear examples.[7]

Although the approach and challenge to addressing a motivational issue rather than an ability issue may vary, they both have one thing in common: Expectations aren't being met.

Raised Expectations

Sometimes expectations are not explicit but rather implied because of certain actions or events. Dante has been with the organization since it began and has shared in its growth. He's done a great job as the accounting director and has always received positive feedback. He aspires to become CFO and has an expectation that he'll be considered for that role when it becomes available. The CEO has a discussion with Dante explaining that although he has good accounting skills and has been successful in his current role, he needs to gain more finance experience. They work out a development plan to prepare Dante for a future promotion.

You place job listings and recruitment advertisements soliciting job candidates and you receive resumes. You solicit a service provider or consultant and receive proposals. Though you can't choose them all, you've raised expectations that they'll at least receive a response. Of course, you notify the successful candidates, but what about the unsuccessful ones? Be respectful of people's time and efforts and close the loop; let the unsuccessful candidates know they were not selected.

> **Don't create a ball of confusion**. Max always assigned tasks to his staff. When they gave the completed assignment to him, he'd ask, "Why are you giving me this?" They learned not to start the task until he asked for it several times.

The Right Approach

Violet was surprised to hear that some of her coworkers thought that Enrique's approach in describing the policy change was too blunt. She interpreted it as factual and direct. What is the right approach and can you use the same approach with everyone? In a *Harvard Business Review* article, "How to Coach, According to 5 Great Sports Coaches," different approaches are discussed. Sir Alex Ferguson, coach of Manchester United, says that "few people get better" with criticism; most respond to encouragement instead." American football coach Bill Parcells, famous for turning around under-performing teams, prefers brutal honesty, saying, "You have to tell them the truth about their performance, you have to tell it to them face-to-face, and you have to tell it to them over and over again."

A more balanced approach comes from Bill Walsh, the business-like coach of three Super Bowl-winning 1980s San Francisco 49ers football teams. He compared two of his most famous quarterbacks, Joe Montana and Steve Young, who were at opposite ends of the spectrum and adapted his style to meet their individual needs. He was careful to nurture Joe to use his instincts, whereas he had to work with Steve to be disciplined enough not to overuse his instincts and stay within the framework of what the team was doing. Bela Karolyi, the gymnastics coach, also tailored his approach to the situation. "Criticism and encouragement have to be alternated and used at the right time and in the right situation."[8]

Both Bill Walsh and Bela Karolyi were implementing the Hersey/Blanchard Situational Leadership Model. Ken Blanchard and Paul Hersey based their model on the theory that instead of using just one style, successful leaders change their leadership styles based on factors such as the situation, the details of the task, and their relationships with the people they are leading. The four main leadership styles are telling (or directing), selling (or coaching), participating (or supporting), and delegating.[9]

➡ Appendix: Hersey/Blanchard Situational
Leadership Model

To his credit, Enrique took the time to know his staff members and he often took different approaches with different individuals. However, in the staff meeting when he discussed the paid time off policy, he used the approach he felt best met the situation directing. He had to make a decision and provide specific instructions.

Confronting the Boss

The Situational Leadership Model can be applied to conflict management, and you need not have a formal title of "leader" to apply it. An individual can lead from any chair. Regardless of their position in the organization, they can effectively manage conflict.

Sandy works for Boris, a micromanager. She proposes a new process to him that will allow invoices to be prepared in a more efficient manner, but it means that he'll have to relinquish some control to Sandy. It worked for a few days until he began hovering over Sandy's desk, checking and rechecking her work; fearful, Sandy suspected, that she'll make a mistake. Although Sandy is uncomfortable confronting Boris, she knows he wants a take-charge person, someone who is firm and declarative. It is not Sandy's nature to be direct, but she understands that this is the way Boris wants to be treated. As difficult as it is for Sandy, she suggests to Boris that he let her do her work without interference so she can finish in a timely manner. This will give him more time to spend on other projects. If after two weeks the new process is not working or if she's making mistakes, then they can decide together on a new course of action. If her work is relatively error-free, it will be much easier for both of them.[10]

Remember Claire and Jacob from Chapter 4? She needs to confront Jacob in order to set some expectations, but she knows that she needs to do it in a manner to which he'll respond and respect. Jacob came from a very hierarchical organization where the chain of control trumped all other factors. The organization where they both work now has a matrix structure and reporting relationships are more fluid. However, even in a matrix structure, order and discipline are valued. That's the hook she'll need to use to get his attention.

When she approaches Jacob and requests a meeting, he's aloof and indifferent, but nevertheless agrees. She begins by explaining that she was on a weekly status call with the client and that he interrupted her at a pivotal moment when she was giving her update. She explains the impact his behavior had on her: It was difficult for her to concentrate while he paced in her office and she was concerned that the client would perceive her as hesitant and unprepared. If they perceived she was not confident, would they think she lacked the discipline for this rigorous project? Claire had assumed the role of leader and was employing the directive style.

As Jacob responds to Claire, she switches her leadership style to selling as she explains how their organization is structured and operates. In this matrix structure, she's accountable to the client, to the project leader, and to him, stressing that their clients value order and discipline from the firm as their service provider. Acknowledging that this environment is different than the ones in which he's used to working, Claire switches her style once again to be participating and suggests that they collaborate to set mutual expectations for working with each other. Jacob agrees and asks if they can set a meeting for the next day so he has some time to prepare.

Expectations play a critical role in conflict management. Setting and adhering to expectations can prevent a conflict or keep it from escalating. Expectations provide a set of standards and make people accountable and help maintain constructive relationships at work. When expectations are not met, facts should be presented showing how the behavior or performance didn't measure up, diffusing any potential confrontation by making it difficult to refute the facts. Take the initiative to make things better and lead by example.

Essential Tips

* People want to know what's expected of them. Tell them early and tell them often.

* Be accountable for the expectations you set and hold others accountable as well.

* Change behavior by pointing out natural consequences—the impact of the actions on others.

* Expectations can be implied as well as expressed. When you've raised expectations through your actions, don't keep people hanging. Close the loop.

* Adjust your leadership style to the situation and the people involved.

* Don't be afraid to lead from any chair in the organization.

CHAPTER 7

DON'T DRAW A LINE IN THE SAND!

I don't know exactly where ideas come from, but when I'm working well, ideas just appear. I've heard other people say similar things—so it's one of the ways I know there's help and guidance out there. It's just a matter of figuring out how to receive the ideas or information that are waiting to be heard.

—Jim Henson

It's time for performance appraisals and salary decisions. Ron, the manager, comes to talk to Celine, the HR director, about one of his employees, Megan, whom he describes as an outstanding performer. Ron proposes giving her a 7-percent increase because she's a "hard worker." Celine responds that the salary increase budget is 3 percent this year and that if he exceeds that for one employee, he'll have to take it away from someone else, assuming he wants to give everyone a 3-percent increase. Ron proposes that Celine meet him halfway, split the difference, and give Megan a 5-percent increase, thinking to himself that if Celine agrees, that's more than the 4.5 percent he originally was going to propose. He sits back in the chair thinking that he's done a good job negotiating this deal.

Was what Ron doing negotiating, or was he merely bargaining from a position? Was he solving the issue of recognizing his outstanding performer? In their book, *Getting to Yes,* Roger Fisher and William Ury present a four-step process for negotiating issues:

* ❊ "Separate the people from the problem.
* ❊ Focus on interests, not positions.
* ❊ Create options.
* ❊ Insist on using objective criteria."[1]

When you're in a conflict, you're problem solving. You're identifying, addressing, and resolving issues just as you are in a negotiation. The same four-step process applies. The people issues involved in conflict and problem solving have been explored in earlier chapters. We're going to take a look at the rest of the steps in the process in this chapter.

Focus on Interests, Not Positions

A position is a stand we take in an argument, negotiation, or conflict. It is what we demand from the other person(s). Interests are what we really want: our needs, desires, and concerns. When positions become the focus of the conflict, the problem can get covered up along with any useful solution.

Consider the following:

Dale's boss makes the following statement to him: "This is not the type of work I'm used to seeing from you. Maybe the project needs to be assigned to someone else."[2] Dale's boss is obviously not pleased, but what is his true interest? Does he really want to take the project from Dale, or is that the *position* he is taking? Isn't what he needs Dale to do—his interest—is to improve his work?

Lenora is feeling a great deal of pressure now that her daughter is in grade school and becoming more involved in activities. Lenora's husband travels frequently for his job, leaving her with the primary responsibility of getting their daughter to and from child care before and after school. She enjoys her job and the company she works for, but she's considering leaving and looking for part-time work. That's the position she's leaning toward, but her underlying interest is to have more flexibility and strike a good work-life balance.

Lixin is a Web developer whose performance has been good, but she needs more growth opportunity. She is placed onto a new project that gives her the chance to develop new skills necessary to advance. Brad, her supervisor, has received feedback from Arne, the project leader, about Lixin's interaction with the new client. Arne indicated that Lixin's communication skills are poor and that she doesn't come to meetings prepared to discuss items on the agenda. He's hinting that he wants her off the project because she's a poor reflection on the team. Brad is adamant that he wants Lixin to stay. From past experience, he knows she's always prepared and has no trouble communicating.

In any conflict, think about what your interest is and then separate your position from your interest. In other words, don't draw a line in the sand! Be able to articulate your interest or interests to yourself and to the others involved, and to explain why it's important to you. Be excited about your interests and make them come alive. When you discuss them with the others, be specific and give good information. Making your interests come alive will increase the likelihood that the other side will agree that your interests are important. It will help to move the discussion away from positions.

Trying to determine and articulate your interests to yourself is often the first battle you have in a conflict. This may be a good time for you to *go to the balcony*. In negotiations, the balcony is often used as a metaphor for a detached state of mind where you can see a scene clearly from afar. It's a place of perspective, calm, and clarity.[3] Going to the balcony is a technique often used when you need to take time out, for example, when you're in a heated argument. Remember Victor from Chapter 4. He wanted to take a break, cool off, and have some time to reflect. The balcony can also be a place you go to in order to prepare before you even enter a discussion or bring up an issue that could lead to conflict. It gives you the opportunity to assess and evaluate the situation objectively, just like an outside party might do.

When you give yourself the time to reflect on your interests, you also want to be thinking about the interests of the other side. In Chapter 2 we discussed learning more about the other person so we can better understand their story.

➡ Chapter 2: Why Can't Everyone Be Like Me?

If you take the time to look at the situation from their perspective, to stand in their shoes, it will give you the opportunity to contemplate what they really want; that is, their interests. Think about the position they've taken and then ask yourself why they might be making this demand. What might it be that they really want? Underlying your interests and their interests are both individuals' needs and values. If you can gain a mutual understanding of those interests, a better understanding of each other's story, you can begin to make informed decisions and be better equipped to create options to resolve the conflict.

> Remember Jack and Kate from Chapter 2? They were part of a team that develops products. Jack will promise anything to make the client happy and Kate is most concerned with product excellence. They usually argue from their positions: relationships vs. quality. Beyond their positions, their shared interest is customer satisfaction.

When Brad sits down to talk with Lixin to discuss the feedback he received from Arne, he learns that she's upset, but not surprised at the feedback. She recognizes that the assignment is a stretch for her and it's the first time she's had the opportunity to interact directly with a client. However, she's receiving little guidance from Arne and often hears about client meetings at the last minute, giving her no time to prepare. That's why she's communicating so poorly, and she knows it's a bad reflection on the team and the project. She's frustrated that she's not being given the visibility or level of technical responsibility she expected. She can't work with Arne and wants to be reassigned.

Brad quickly realizes that there are a number of issues involved in this situation. He has to separate them and then determine what everyone may want. Both he and Lixin are interested in developing her technical skills—one mutual interest. Brad, Lixin, and Arne all want the project to be a success—another mutual interest. However, Brad is not certain if Arne has a more primary interest, namely using this assignment to advance his own career. If that's the case, he'll have to deal with that issue separately. Isolating the issues and the interests associated with each will help Brad address these conflicts.

➡ Appendix: Position vs. Interest—An Exercise

Let's go back and see how Ron and Celine are doing. As Ron sits back smugly in his chair, Celine is thinking that there are budget constraints and published guidelines for managers to adhere to in making salary decisions. She wants to be fair to everyone—that's her interest. Ron has already made it clear that he wants to give Megan a much larger raise and not take money away from other employees in order to do so—that's his position. Celine can't help but wonder why. What's the underlying reason that he's taking this stance? "Ron," she says, "I know that you want to be fair to everyone; so do I. If I agreed to let every manager do what you're proposing, it would bankrupt us. I know Megan's a hard worker, but so are your other employees. What's really going on?" Ron confesses he's concerned that Megan may be looking for another job and he doesn't want to lose her. She's got very strong skills, takes the lead on tackling tough tasks, and gets along so well with everyone. Now Ron and Celine are on the same page—their mutual interests are employee recognition and retention. Realizing that neither wants to lose Megan, they are ready to move to the next step: creating options for mutual gain.

Create Options

Ron may have thought he was "negotiating" with Celine when he suggested that she meet him halfway in determining the raise to give Megan. However, problem solving is not meeting someone halfway, nor is it making an either/or proposition.

When the people involved in a conflict stay locked in their positions, they tend to think that there are only two solutions to the problem: the one that's good for them and the one that's good for the other person. This stifles any creative thinking. If you take the approach that Ron did, splitting the difference, people are then encouraged to ask for more than they really want and can make unreasonable demands. In fact, that's exactly what Ron did. He really wanted to give Megan a 4.5-percent increase, but he started by asking for a 7-percent increase.

Problem solving involves finding creative solutions that satisfy all identified interests—mutual or otherwise—of all the parties. When you move the discussion away from positions and start exploring interests, as Celine did, you recognize that there is a mutual problem (not his, not hers), and your collective focus should be solving that problem. Knowing that there was a risk of losing a valued employee, Celine and Ron were able to propose several options that would recognize Megan's contributions:

* Celine suggested giving Megan a combination salary increase of 3 percent and an additional bonus of 2 percent. Because the bonus was a one-time event, it wouldn't escalate her salary beyond the standard.

* Ron suggested that he could send her to a conference to represent the organization. This would recognize her hard work.

* A new project was being awarded to the company and Ron could assign Megan to it, which would give her more visibility.

As Rosamund Stone Zander and Benjamin Zander write, invent possibilities by asking yourself: "What assumption am I making,/ That I'm not aware I'm making,/That gives me what I see?" And when you have an answer, ask yourself: "What might I now invent,/That I haven't yet invented,/That would give me other choices?"[4]

When Jack and Kate stopped bickering and recognized that their shared interest was customer satisfaction, they were better able to focus on the client. They had to determine the client's interest. Jack believed that the client wanted the product customized or tailored to its needs. Kate pointed out that if they did this, it would result in a substantial cut in the company's profits and Jack's commission. She saw two options which she discussed with Jack:

✳ If the client wants a customized *design*, are they willing to pay a higher price for the additional costs associated with tailoring the product to their specific needs?

✳ Would the customer be willing to explore a solution using off-the-shelf components that would give them a customized *product* for their needs without incurring the significant cost increase?

Too often problem solving is done in an unfocused way. Emotions take over or solutions are offered before interests are clearly identified. Remember the discussions in Chapter 4 about having effective conversations and getting and giving good information?

Celine and Kate both took the opportunity to go to the balcony and cleared their heads to gain the perspective they needed to see options from an unbiased viewpoint. When Celine did it and started presenting options to Ron, it sparked his creativity. Her focus brought him into focus. Whether she realized it or not, Celine started a brainstorming session with Ron.

Brainstorming is an excellent technique to use to create options and engage in imaginative thinking. In brainstorming, anything goes and any idea is acceptable. For brainstorming to be successful the people involved must agree on the problem to be addressed; multiple problems or interests may require separate brainstorming sessions. Everyone has to agree to the following guidelines:

1. Any and all ideas are encouraged, no matter how unconventional or wild they may appear. The objective is to generate as many ideas as possible.

2. No idea is criticized or evaluated during the process. This is the Golden Rule of brainstorming. Evaluating the ideas comes later.

3. All ideas that are offered are written down. Nothing is discounted or ignored.

After the brainstorming session, useful ideas can be highlighted and discussed. This can occur in another meeting.

Brad met with both Lixin and Arne separately. Confident that the issue they had in common was client satisfaction, he then brought them together for a brainstorming session. He reviewed the guidelines for the session and asked them to each state the problem as they saw it. They were all in agreement that they wanted to ensure the project's success and deliver a quality solution to the client. Here are some of the ideas that they generated:

✳ More frequent team meetings to provide status updates and briefings regarding information Arne had received from his daily meetings with the client.

* Daily e-mail updates from Arne to the team.

* Bi-weekly meetings between Lixin and Arne to discuss technical details and feedback.

* Weekly meetings between Brad and Arne regarding team performance and individual member performance.

* Coaching sessions between Brad and Arne to develop his people management skills.

* Allow Lixin to attend client meetings with Arne so she can have firsthand information and better understand the client's needs.

* Meetings between Lixin and Arne prior to client presentations so he can critique her reports and provide feedback.

* Assign Lixin to work with another team member in a peer-to-peer mentoring arrangement.

Brad is pleased that so many good ideas were generated. Just as he had hoped, there were several options that could work rather than opposing options and points of view. He asks that they all break for a few hours and come back in the afternoon so they can begin evaluating the ideas and come up with some good alternatives. He knows that there are other interests he'll have to work on with Lixin and Arne independently, but this brainstorming session has been a real breakthrough.

Objective Criteria

The last step in the process of coming up with a solution to the problem or conflict is to identify objective criteria against which options and/or potential solutions can be evaluated. Objective criteria are independent of each person's will, and are practical, relevant, and legitimate. How do you develop and use objective criteria? Think in advance about fair standards and fair procedures. Fair standards are based on things such as market value, precedent, professional standards, scientific judgment, or equal treatment.[5] Safety or quality standards are examples of fair and independent standards. Objective criteria can also include precedent, efficiency, and costs.

> Ivan calls HR about Vanessa who's been missing time at work. She's been coming in late and leaving early to visit with her grandmother, who's in the hospital. Although she didn't raise her, Vanessa is very close to her grandmother, who needs emotional support right now. Ivan wants to submit the paperwork to put Vanessa on a family medical leave. Perry, the HR manager, explains that the situation doesn't meet the standards in the law. Whereas family medical leave is available to care for a spouse, parent, or child but generally not a grandmother (fair standard), the organization could arrange for a 30-day personal leave if Vanessa wanted to consider it (creative option).

> Meanwhile, Perry is addressing Jackie's concern. Jackie protested providing forms completed by her doctor to HR in order to be considered for a family medical leave, Perry had to explain to her that the process was in place to ensure her right to take the job-protected leave (fair procedure).

Objective criteria should appeal and relate to shared interests and shared standards. Shared interests can be common interests of the larger community, such as the company or the industry in which the company operates, as well as the mutual interests of the individuals involved in the conflict. Objective criteria can be based on shared standards or values, such as equality, fairness, integrity, or quality.[6] Remember the discussions in Chapter 2 about culture and cultural variables. Most importantly, the criteria must be fair and reasonable, and often there are many relevant criteria. For that reason, you should research in advance which might best apply, show why those criteria more favorable to you are more relevant, and show why those less favorable to you are less relevant.[7]

Consider the following examples in which fair and reasonable standards were applied:

A small consulting firm had a re-occurring project with a client. Every year when it came time to do the work, the client would complain about the price, which was always the same, and ask for a discount. The president of the consulting firm had to remind the client that the price they were being charged was the same price that other clients with the same size project were charged. If they gave this client a discount, it would not be fair to all the others.

Raphael had worked hard on a paper presenting the findings from research he had done for a new program his organization was about to implement. He was going to present the paper at an industry conference. He was approached by Sheila, a vice president in his organization, who asked him if she could present the paper on behalf of the company and be named as a contributing author, even though she was not part of the research team, nor had any involvement with the program. His mind raced through a multiple of possible responses, but he knew he did not want to compromise his values. He responded, "I'm afraid I can't do that."

Organizations develop policies and procedures to establish objective criteria for handling a wide range of management issues, such as how people are hired, paid, or promoted, which travel expenses are allowable, and how to procure outside goods and services, just to name a few. Through policies and practices, organizations can set a framework for treating people with respect and fairness. Many times policies represent the organization's response to the external environment, such as laws and regulations, and can offer a degree of legal protection to the employer and employee alike. Policies should reflect the culture and values of the organization, set and communicate expectations, and assure consistency in the way people are treated.[8]

When Lenora comes rushing into the office late one morning, her stress is at a high level. Her daughter was especially cranky this morning and they were late leaving the house. Her boss, Angela, can't help but notice her tension and comes to see what the problem is. Lenora confesses she needs more balance in her life and is looking for part-time work. Angela is concerned and they begin to talk through options. The company is going to start a pilot telecommuting program in just a few weeks and Angela thinks that Lenora would be a good candidate because she meets the criteria for the program. The nature of her job is fairly independent, and she can connect virtually with others in the office. Lenora is self-motivated, has good time management skills, is familiar with the work and the company, and is a valued eorgamployee.[9] Although she can't guarantee that this will be a permanent solution, Angela encourages Lenora to seriously consider this. They need employees like Lenora to make the program a success. Lenora quickly realizes that she's fortunate to work in a job and in an industry where flexibility can be offered.

Lela had decided to strike out on her own and do freelance work. When she received a call from her former boss asking if she'd be available for a project, Lela jumped at the opportunity. He offered to pay her the same hourly amount that he'd pay to an employment agency that might provide a contractor. Lela's hourly rate was about 35 percent higher. She reminded him that, as she'd worked for the firm before and was familiar with their processes, she could get the work done in half the time that another contractor would take. She pointed out that she'd be the more cost-effective option for him. It didn't take him long to agree.

Salary decisions, like the situation between Celine and Ron, should always be based on objective criteria. Savvy organizations benchmark their pay practices against external standards, especially those in their industries. They conduct salary surveys to see what other similar organizations are paying for similar jobs. In determining salary increases, a matrix is often used that considers an employee's pay in relation to the job's pay grade and the employee's performance rating. This was the standard to which Celine was holding Ron accountable. She was also considering what other employees in Ron's department with the similar experience and performance history were making and how much of an increase they'd receive. She wanted to make sure that all of the salary increases were fair and consistent.

Drawing a line in the sand and arguing from one side of the line or the other will not resolve a conflict; it will only exacerbate the situation. Resolving conflict means that you have to be tough on the problem, but soft on the people. The people involved have to move off of their positions and identify and satisfy all the interests. Creative alternatives and solutions based on the interest need to be devised and the final agreement must be fair, reasonable, and objective.

Essential Tips

❋ Focus on the problem and not the people involved in the conflict. Stand in the other people's shoes and look at the problem from their perspective. Strive to maintain good relationships.

* Interests help you see the real problem. Identify all of the interests of all of the parties to the conflict.

* Go to the balcony to see things from a different perspective. It will help you to gain clarity.

* Imagine that anything is possible. It will help you to invent the most creative options. Some of the best solutions have come from wild ideas.

* After a brainstorming session, take some time before you evaluate the ideas.

* Use objective criteria to evaluate those ideas. If you do so, it is more likely that the solutions will be good for and fair to both sides.

CHAPTER 8

WHAT'S YOUR TYPE?

If two people on the job agree all the time, then one is useless. If they disagree all the time, then both are useless.

—Dale Carnegie

In order to manage conflict in the workplace, it is important to be able to understand and adjust to the situation. What is the source of the tension? How do the people involved in the conflict (including you) respond to conflict?

Each of us has a conflict style preference. As Mitchell and Gamlem say in *The Big Book of HR*:

There are five recognized modes for dealing with conflict that describe an individual's behavior along two basic dimensions: (1) assertiveness, the extent to which the person attempts to satisfy his own concerns, and (2) cooperativeness, the extent to which the person attempts to satisfy the other person's concerns.

* Competing—attacks and likes to argue and debate. This type is competitive, assertive, and uncooperative, and can be threatening and intimidating, causing others to give in to avoid the argument. The competing type takes the stance of "win or lose," often pursuing his/her own concerns, at the other person's expense. Competing means "standing up for your rights," defending a position you believe is correct, or simply trying to win.

* Accommodating is unassertive and cooperative, and is the complete opposite of competing. When accommodating, the individual neglects his/her own concerns because of high levels of concern about others. This type needs to please and be liked by others. Accommodating might take the form of yielding to another's point of view, or giving in during disagreements even when he/she believes his/her ideas are better.

* Avoiding is unassertive and uncooperative; this person neither pursues his/her own

concerns nor those of the other individual. This type will not commit and is unsure where he/she stands on issues. Often, he/she conceals his/her interests until a better time, or simply withdraws from a threatening situation.

* Collaborating is both assertive and cooperative—the complete opposite of avoiding, takes a win-win stance, and involves an attempt to work with others to find some solution that fully satisfies his/her concerns. This style approaches conflict with skill and balance, understands the value of positive conflict, and often acts as a mediator. Collaborating means exploring the issues and working to find a creative solution.

* Compromising is moderate in both assertiveness and cooperativeness. The objective is to find some expedient, mutually acceptable solution that partially satisfies both parties. It falls between competing and accommodating. Compromise gives up more than competing but less than accommodating. Likewise, it addresses an issue more directly than avoiding, but does not explore it in as much depth as collaborating. This type is intimidated by direct confrontation and will look to gain consensus or seek a quick middle-ground solution.

> Each of us is capable of using all five conflict-handling modes. None of us can be characterized as having a single style of dealing with conflict. But certain people use some modes better than others and, therefore, tend to rely on those modes more heavily than others—whether because of temperament or practice.[1]

Marina loves the give and take of a good argument. Any time she can feel as if she is the winner and someone else is the loser, she is a happy employee. She was on the debate team in college and learned all the techniques of rebutting the position or argument of the other person involved in the conflict. She will avoid at all costs doing what she considers "giving in" to the point of the other person or people involved. Others on the team find her intimidating and sometimes even threatening. Her conflict style is competing.

Jackson is what is commonly called a "people pleaser." He wants everyone to like him, so he bends over backward to do whatever it takes to have peace and harmony on the team. He is concerned about never doing anything that might hurt someone else's feelings, so he doesn't let anyone know how he really feels about the issues during a conflict. He would rather give in to someone else on the team so as not to upset them, even if he is pretty sure he has a better idea than the one they've presented. Jackson is loved by all because he makes sure everyone else wins in conflicts. He is especially popular with people like Marina who have to win no matter what! His style is accommodating.

Leeann runs as fast as she can when she sees a conflict coming—be it on the team or with her manager or her family. Because she won't enter a conflict, no one else in the department knows where she stands or how she really feels. She hides her feelings and her positions on issues so that no one will want to engage her in a discussion or a debate. Even when she is asked for an opinion, she hedges, saying things like, "I really don't have an opinion on that." Leeann is extremely uncomfortable with Marina and others who have her competing style, but loves to work with people like Jackson who won't ever try to find out what she really thinks. Her style is avoiding.

Dev often plays the role of mediator or peacekeeper on the team or in the department because he understands that conflict can be valuable and move the team or work group forward. He is a good listener and practices the active listening principles outlined in Chapter 5 of this book. Dev recognizes the conflict style of others and is able to use that knowledge to bring people together. He is very self-aware and has a high degree of emotional intelligence; therefore, he is able to manage his emotions. Even Marina works well with Dev because she knows he understands her need to win while helping her see the big picture. Dev is the one people go to when they want to resolve conflict. His style is collaborating.

Walter doesn't like direct confrontations. He would rather work behind the scenes to find out how others feel. He has a strong need to think things through before getting involved in the issues. He is really good at building consensus because he has solicited opinions from others before helping the team or the department to reach the "middle ground." Marina, Jackson, Leeann, and Dev can all work with Walter and he is most help-ful in building consensus. His style is compromising.

Understanding Your Style

As Lynne Eisaguirre writes in *The Power of a Good Fight*, "It is important to realize that none of these styles are right or wrong. They are simply examples of style. The key is to try and increase the different styles we want to use to skillfully resolve conflict, solve prob-lems more creatively, and prepare more effectively for the future."[2]

Understanding your own preferred conflict style and the preferred conflict style of others can really help take some emotion and some personalization out of the conflict. When we understand conflict styles, we hopefully will stop thinking in terms of "I'm right and he's wrong," and take the actions of others less person-ally. Then we can use the energy we'd normally waste on trying to figure them out to creatively resolve the underlying issues of the dispute. We can also con-sciously choose to use a different conflict style when the situation demands it, but it takes practice to use a style that perhaps isn't as comfortable for you as your preferred style. However, you can learn to use different styles effectively and it is worth it to try!

Here are some ideas for you to consider once you know your own preferred conflict style in order to max-imize your effectiveness when dealing with conflict.

If your preferred style is competing, you probably consider yourself to be courageous. So, if you truly are courageous, do you have the ability to reveal the un-derlying fear or hurt to the person with whom you are in conflict? If you do, you may be really surprised and pleased to find better ways to communicate that will help you to embrace conflict rather than attacking it. You may find you are able to use the energy you once spent on being confrontational to work collaboratively. As a result, conflict is transformed to creativity. So, when conflict arises:

※ Stop, breathe, and count to 10.

※ Try to understand the underlying fear or feelings of the other(s).

※ Ask yourself:

    ○ What am I afraid of here?

    ○ What am I afraid of losing or what losses have I already suffered?

    ○ Am I feeling hurt or is what's happening that is reminding me of past hurts?

※ Write down all your thoughts about the issue once you've identified your fears/hurts and then ask:

    ○ Is this the best way to come to agreement?

    ○ Am I willing to use this conflict to spark creativity rather than indulging in my need to run over others' interests?

    ○ Can I learn to engage in creative dialogue rather than a win/lose debate?

    ○ Will what I'm doing alleviate my fear?

※ Learn to appreciate how others approach conflict.

If your conflict style is accommodating, you need to be aware that taking care of yourself is a key because you are highly susceptible to burnout. Remember what the flight attendants say at the beginning of every flight: "In case of a sudden drop in altitude, oxygen masks will fall from above your head. Put your own mask on first before helping others." This simply means that you can't be everything to everyone—you have to take care of yourself! This is not selfish; it is just good common sense. So, when conflict occurs:

* Monitor your reactions to be sure you are doing what you want to do.

* Learn to reveal who you really are.

* Ask for what you need. If you can't take this step, you won't be able to creatively embrace the conflict.

* Don't think you have to be cheerful all the time unless this is how you really feel.

* Honor your own needs rather than just trying to please others.

* Learn to actively participate in the process of innovative dialogue.

* Learn to appreciate how others approach conflict.

If your conflict style is avoiding, you may constantly wonder how you manage to attract so many angry, resentful, sad, or worried people. Here's why: they are simply expressing the emotions you won't own. You need to acknowledge that your preferred conflict style is to avoid it and you need to consciously consider, as Dr. Phil says, "How's this working for you?"

When conflict comes up:

* Start appropriately revealing your own feelings.

✳ Start owning your feelings.

✳ Find ways to express how you feel.

✳ Learn to value conflict.

✳ Learn to appreciate how others approach conflict.

✳ Learn to manage your own emotions so that you can sustain your own participation in the messy process of working through a conflict.

✳ Learn to use conflict creatively instead of feeling abused by its very existence.

If your conflict style is compromising, you need to try to develop the ability to act on your convictions; be courageous and:

✳ Value the conflict and recognize its creative potential.

✳ Find a way to skillfully communicate your needs and interests.

✳ Find a way to talk with the people involved in the issue.

✳ Learn how to talk to people directly.

✳ Consider what your role is in the situation and how you can have impact.

If your conflict style is collaborating, you need to recognize your value and your strengths when conflict occurs in your workplace and:

✳ Offer to mediate when conflicts come up in your workplace.

✳ Continue to hone your listening skills and your ability to control your emotions.

Each of us is capable of using all five conflict-handling modes. None of us can be characterized as having a single style of dealing with conflict. But, certain people use some modes better than others and, therefore, tend to rely on those modes more heavily than others whether because of temperament or practice.[3]

➡   Appendix: Discovering Your Conflict Style

Working With Other Styles

Now that you understand your own preferred style of dealing with conflict, it will be helpful to try to understand the people you work with and how they approach conflict. Although it's probably not a great idea to just ask them, if you listen carefully and observe your coworkers, you will probably be able to get a pretty good idea of their conflict mode. Once you're armed with that knowledge (and remember: Just like you, other people may use different conflict modes at different times), here are some ideas of how you can work successfully with a person using that particular conflict style or mode:

If you're working with someone whose style preference is competing, take time to allow them to vent. You will want to be gracious while doing your best to discover what they fear. This is a good place for you to use the reflective listening skills you learned in Chapter 5. And don't forget that humor may go a long way in getting a competing person to relax and then be able to resolve the conflict.

If you're working with someone whose style preference is avoiding, you will need to be direct and patient while you work to understand their position. You will need to be supportive and allow that person to feel as if they can confront you with their issue.

If you're working with someone whose style preference is compromising, the active listening skills you learned in Chapter 5 will be useful as you work to create a supportive environment where the person will feel comfortable. Try describing the impact of their behavior on the situation and allow them to feel as if they can confront you with the issue.

If you're working with someone who is accommodating, you need to try and get them to open up on how they are feeling and what they fear. You need to monitor their energy level because they are susceptible to burnout. Your role is to solicit their input and their feedback, as they probably won't offer it willingly.

If you're working with someone whose style preference is collaborating, you and others in your work group will probably learn early on to depend on them in conflict situations because they are skilled at resolving whatever comes up. Watch and learn from them in order to enhance your own abilities to deal with conflict.

In conclusion, why is it so important to understand our own conflict style preference and the style preferences of those around us? Different styles lead to different approaches to how we relate to others and how we work together. These style preferences aren't perfect or always accurate, but can be helpful as you work with others in your organization to resolve the conflicts that arise just because we're human beings who think and act differently.

152 THE ESSENTIAL WORKPLACE CONFLICT HANDBOOK

Essential Tips

* ✳ Each of us has a conflict style preference; learn to understand yours and the preferred style of others you work with.

* ✳ Each style has its strengths and weaknesses.

* ✳ Learn to use the most effective style for the situation.

CHAPTER 9

WHOSE FIGHT IS IT ANYWAY?

Knowing when to walk away is wisdom. Being able to is courage. Walking away with your head held high is dignity.

—Anonymous

Remember The Hyde Company from Chapter 1? They moved into a new, wonderfully designed office building with open space to allow for collaboration and private meeting rooms. The well-designed work spaces allow for individual privacy. This is a huge change for the workforce who'd been working in private offices in their old building. Carlo and Bethany have workspaces next to each other. Bethany is having a difficult time adjusting to the new work environment and Carlo is not making things any easier. He has a loud voice that carries, constantly barges into her space, and interrupts her when she's on the phone. She often goes into one of the small private meeting rooms to get away from him. The problem is those rooms have glass walls; Carlo can see her and seek her out for questions. Exasperated, Bethany goes to Sheila, their manager, and asks her to do something with Carlo because he's creating a disruptive and hostile work environment.

➡ Chapter 1: What's New at Work?

Before she decides on a course of action, Sheila needs to learn the nature of Carlo's behavior to determine if it might be some form of workplace harassment.

➡ Chapter 10: Are You Playing Nice in the Sandbox?

Assuming that harassment is not an issue in this situation, then she has to consider the following:

* Who owns this particular conflict?

* If she takes steps to resolve the problem, could she be perceived as taking sides with Bethany?

* If she steps in and exerts her authority, will Bethany miss the opportunity to develop her own conflict-management skills?

* As the company is encouraging more collaboration among its employees, will she dilute their ability to do so if she solves the problem for them?

Sheila is aware that Carlo's voice projects and in the open space, it can sound louder than he intends. Bethany, on the other hand, is often slow getting Carlo what he needs, which frustrates him. What Sheila sees is a third story: a non-judgmental, unbiased view of what's occurring between Bethany and Carlo. Sheila has an interest in the conflict because it involves two of her team members, but she doesn't own it. She can, however, take some action to bring it to a resolution. She can act as a mediator.

Learning to Mediate

Mediators are third parties who help people solve their problems. They help people in conflict find their own solutions. Think of a marriage counselor, mutual friend or peer, HR professional, manager, or team leader—these are people who may be called upon because they have the vantage point of a neutral observer.

Mediation is facilitated negotiation and, as we pointed out in Chapter 7, negotiation is problem solving. Mediation is an approach to resolving conflict that does not involve an imposed solution. The people involved decide how the problem will be solved and any resolution achieved is consensual. One positive outcome of mediation is that it encourages communication. Everyone involved has an opportunity to better understand the other sides and the other stories. Additional issues may surface that provide greater insight. The exchange of information in a cooperative manner strengthens working relationships. Another positive outcome is that the process helps develop problem-solving skills for those involved in the conflict.

Sheila understands that, as a mediator, the option of resolving the problem herself is eliminated. The solution must come from Bethany and Carlo. She also understands that she has the ability to see the third story. She can describe the problem in a way that rings true for both of them.[1] She can move them toward a more collaborative relationship, which supports the company's goal. However, she has to remain objective.

Her next steps will be:

* Defining the business problem that's impacting the workplace and communicating that problem to Bethany and Carlo.

* Scheduling a meeting for the three of them and securing their agreement to attend.

* Defining roles at the beginning of the meeting. She has to be clear that she will be facilitating the discussion between the two of them, and not asking questions or giving advice or opinions, even if she's asked.

* Setting guidelines at the beginning of the meeting. She'll want to encourage Bethany and Carlo to identify their individual interests, ask questions, and propose solutions. Once again, she'll have to be clear that she will not be asking questions nor proposing the solutions. Proposing solutions and agreeing on a resolution is their responsibility.

➡ Chapter 7: Don't Draw a Line in the Sand!

Managers should:

✳ Be sensitive to the working relationships among your team members. You need to be aware of *how* your employees do their jobs, not just *if* they do their jobs.

✳ Be open and encourage team members to talk with you and with each other. You're not responsible for resolving conflicts in which you're not directly involved, but you can make sure that issues are open and not masked.

✳ Gain an understanding of the interests of the parties involved in the conflict. It will help you to be more effective in the event you are called on to mediate.

➡ Appendix: Preparing to Mediate: A Checklist

Who Owns the Conflict?

As we've been observing, workplace conflicts are not simple. The nature of each conflict is unique. There are often several underlying issues resulting in more than one conflict to be resolved. It's important to identify and separate the issues to determine who owns which conflict and how each is best resolved. A guiding principle—in fact a Golden Rule—of conflict resolution is that the problem should be solved by the individuals who own it. Remember Harrison from Chapter 4? He knew he had to have a difficult conversation with Louise and didn't hand it off to someone else.

Randall recently promoted Juanita into a supervisory role giving her responsibility for the work of one employee, Tricia. Juanita doubts that this is positive for her because she has no prior management experience and Randall is not very supportive. Randall told her that Tricia was "unmanageable." Though Tricia is very good at customer service—she supports the organization's patrons and there's a desire by some to retain her—she doesn't take direction well and often has disagreements with her coworkers. If Juanita doesn't accept the promotion and manage her, Tricia will be without a job. Juanita is aware that Tricia has been moved around the organization a great deal. Within a matter of days, Randall advises Juanita that a complaint has been received about Tricia's attitude and that Juanita needs to handle it.

Does Juanita own this problem? Without more information about Tricia's employment history, it's difficult to pinpoint who owns it. Most likely, several people in the past failed to take ownership and passed it on. Unfortunately, it's all too common that problems are ignored, swept aside, or moved around, resulting in larger conflicts. It's very possible that this situation is just a symptom of a larger, systemic problem in this organization.

Renata has an abrasive personality. In meetings, she's especially aggressive, cutting people off when they are talking and making snide remarks about ideas that are presented. Recently, when she was having problems with her computer, she stormed into IT and began to make accusations to Mark that he or someone else from IT had worked on her computer during the night. Before Mark could respond, she threw insults at him and stormed out. Mark sent an e-mail to his manager about the incident and his manager went to talk to Renata's boss, Albert. Albert is well aware of Renata's outbursts, but he is conflict adverse. He has continued to tolerate her behavior because she's such a good performer—thorough, precise, and very creative. In desperation, he takes the situation to his director, Sergio, imploring him to handle Renata and the situation. Who owns this problem?

Sergio realizes that Albert is as much a part of the problem as Renata is. Albert has been failing to manage her behavior and it's now time for Sergio to manage Albert's unwillingness to step up. Sergio explains that he sees their mutual interest in maintaining good working relationships among all the staff in a fast-paced environment and Albert agrees. Sergio points out that the organization has a policy that describes standards of conduct to which all employees must adhere, regardless of level of performance. There is also guidance on corrective action that should be taken to address inappropriate behavior.

The facts supporting Renata's behavior are clear. Mark's complaint, which he relayed in writing, is only one of several written complaints that have been received within the past three months. Clearly, Renata has not been working harmoniously with others and she has ignored feedback given by Albert, which could be considered as insubordination. There is more than enough probable cause to take management action in accordance with the conduct policy and place her on a final written warning advising her that, absent improvement in her behavior, further action will take place.

➡ Chapter 11: What's an Organization to Do?

Recognizing that Albert owns the Renata problem, Sergio insists that Albert prepare the final written warning, with his assistance. He also insists that Albert, along with human resources, deliver it to Renata. He wants to remain in the background in order to discourage Renata from thinking that she can bypass Albert and come directly to him. Albert is reluctant, but he recognizes that he has to step up. He asks Sergio if they can get some coaching for Renata. Before he agrees, Sergio suggests that when Albert and Renata sit down, they do some brainstorming to determine how Renata might work on her attitude. Sergio wants Renata to claim ownership and responsibility of this problem. He wants her to be accountable and live up to expectations.

➡ Chapter 6: You Want Me to Do What?

What is the difference between coaching and counseling?

✳ Coaching is a process to enable learning and development to improve performance or meet career goals.

✳ Counseling is working with an employee to get behavior to change.

Renata must to learn to work better with her peers. Counseling is the help she needs at this time. If she turns her behavior around, then coaching might be appropriate to help her to advance in her career. Albert, however, would benefit from coaching at this time.

At the same time, Sergio recognizes that he owns the problem involving Albert's management skills. He suggests that they have a brainstorming session of their own to come up with some ideas of how to help Albert be less conflict averse. They both own that problem.

I'm Not in It!

As it was yet another day in the cold winter when the county's schools were closed, Karina didn't have a choice but to telecommute. Fortunately, her organization had a liberal telecommuting policy. She had a report that her boss needed her to proofread and edit, and then send off to be printed for a meeting the next day. She knew she could have it finished to get it to printing by the 2:00 p.m. deadline. At 12:30 p.m. she e-mailed it to her boss as well as a coworker, Diego, whom she confirmed was in the office that day. Because the production team required a printed copy as well as a soft copy, Karina asked Diego if he could print the report and submit both the hard and soft copies to the production department by 2:00 p.m. She also left instructions regarding the number of copies she needed, the required binding, and her cell phone number in case there were any questions. Karina also received a confirmation that her e-mail to Diego was delivered and read.

At 4:30 p.m. Karina called Diego to check on the status. Diego's voice froze. He'd been so busy covering for someone on sick leave that he never acted on Karina's request. Karina got extremely upset and began making nasty accusations. Diego responded in kind. At that point, their mutual boss approached and overheard the heated exchange. He'd been in meetings most of the day, but assumed that everything was under control. He was furious to learn what happened and threatened to write both of them up, but not before instructing Diego to call the production department's manager and see if they could get a rush on the job. They could, as long as they get it down right away; he'd have it the next morning in time for the meeting.

Next morning, the blame game between Karina and Diego continues. Brittany, who's always cheerful and concerned about others, sees Karina in the coffee room and asks if everything is okay. Karina lets loose with all of the details about what happened yesterday, pressing Brittany to plead her case to their boss. Brittany takes a step back, looks Karina in the eye and says, "Sorry, Karina, but I'm not in it!" Brittany has the good sense to realize that she didn't own this conflict. It's not her fight and she doesn't want to be involved.

Know When and How to Intervene

Sheila and Sergio are modeling good behavior and setting good examples. Brittany should be recognized (and rewarded) for having the good sense to stay out of other people's conflicts. Knowing when and how to intervene is essential. Unfortunately, not everyone has good sense and that often creates rather than solves problems. Also, certain circumstances require specific actions whereas others require expert help. Let's look at some unique circumstances.

Until recently, Vivian has had a history of good performance as a claims reviewer and processor. She has received awards for her efficiency and low error rate, and is called on to help train new employees. Lately, however, her performance is slipping. She's processing fewer claims and her errors are increasing. Even worse, she's been impatient with her coworkers, snapping at them and accusing them of interfering with her work. Filipe has received the brunt of most of her accusations and his patience has run out. None of these changes have gone unnoticed by Tamera, her supervisor. Tamera knows that she's got to intervene and schedules a time to meet with Vivian.

Tamera starts the meeting by expressing concern about Vivian's declining performance. Before she can share her information, Vivian becomes very defensive and accuses Tamera of being unfair. "After all, I've had the best performance in the department for years. Doesn't that count? And Filipe, his mistakes are impacting my work!" she shouts. Tamera senses that there is something going on in Vivian's life that's contributing to these work problems. She is tempted to ask, but decides not to. Instead, she follows the guidance she has received in management training—stick to the facts. She presents Vivian with the statistics regarding her performance, pointing out that, yes, she'd done great work in the past and that is why there is concern. Tamera also describes several situations where she's observed Vivian making snarky remarks to her peers and shouting at Filipe. Tamera then says to her, "Vivian, I need you to get back on track before your performance goes below acceptable standards. I want to support you and help you correct these problems. That's why I've developed an improvement plan so we can both monitor your progress."

At that point Vivian bursts into tears and confesses that things aren't going well at home: Her husband has moved out, money is tight, and she can't afford to lose her job. Tamera silently sighs with relief, thinking that at least Vivian acknowledges that there is a problem. She tells Vivian that the Employee Assistance Program (EAP) is a resource that can help with her personal problems. Although it's Vivian's decision to take advantage of that support, Tamera advises that she is going to make a management referral to the EAP for Vivian based on her performance and behavior changes.[2] Vivian will still be accountable for improving her performance and behavior. Tamera made a wise decision to let the professionals at the EAP counsel Vivian because the underlying causes of her work issues are personal problems. Her responsibility is to continue to manage Vivian's work.

Rosario and Hilde have been working together for years. Friendly at work, they never see each other outside the workplace. Hilde notices some subtle changes in Rosario; she's not as upbeat and pleasant as usual. When she expresses concern about these changes in her disposition, Rosario confides that she's having problems with her teenage son. Hilde suggests she calls the EAP—in fact, presses her to do so. Rosario adamantly refuses. She doesn't want outside interference with personal problems. Hilde decides to call the EAP on Rosario's behalf and is told that the counselors can't assist unless Rosario calls directly—and in fact, they can't discuss Rosario's problem with her. Hilde is outraged and goes to human resources to complain that the EAP is not providing the service it should and insists that the company make a management referral to the EAP.

Was Hilde right to intervene? No, she doesn't own this problem. Unless Rosario is having performance or behavior problems that are affecting her work, there is no basis for a management referral and if there were, it would have to come from Rosario's manager, not Hilde. The EAP was correct in refusing to discuss Rosario's problem with a coworker.

➥ Chapter 11: What's an Organization to Do?

Ivan's supervisor, Greg has been making unwanted and persistent sexual remarks and advances toward him. Ivan has asked for them to stop, but Greg always responds with flippant remarks like "Loosen up!" or "Chill out. I'm kidding." Exasperated, Ivan takes his concerns to Greg's manager, Mariana. Was Ivan correct in asking Mariana to intervene?

In this case, Greg's behavior—which included unwelcome advances and requests for sexual favors—can be described as sexual harassment and the company not only has a right to know, but a legal obligation to investigate Ivan's complaint.[3] Ivan was not only correct in getting his manager involved in this conflict, it was his legal right to do so.

Savvy organizations recognize that conflict is not always bad. They recognize the characteristics of good conflict and leverage it into innovation and creativity. They encourage their employees to be accountable for their role in a conflict situation and give them the tools to manage and resolve their problems. They empower them to solve their own problems.

Essential Tips

✳ Problem solving does not inherently involve a top-down approach. It's not the manager's role to intervene every time employees clash.

∗   Solving employees' problems for them reduces collaboration and makes them dependent on their manager.

∗   Conflict can be change trying to happen. Help your employees develop conflict management skills.

∗   Conflict may not be essential in the workplace, but being accountable and solving your own problems is.

∗   Know when to intervene and know when to walk away.

CHAPTER 10

ARE YOU PLAYING NICE IN THE SANDBOX?

All I really need to know about how to live and what to do and how to be I learned in kindergarten.... Play fair.... Don't hit people.... Clean up your own mess.... Say you're sorry when you hurt somebody....

—Robert Fulghum

Remember a time when someone made you feel respected. Did they listen to you, giving you their undivided attention? Perhaps they valued your opinion even if it differed from their own. Did they provide feedback in an honest and non-judgmental way? Did their actions show consideration?

167

These are a sampling of workplace behaviors that are respectful.

Imagine an organization that defines its values through behaviors that exemplify them, where leaders and associates all live those values, and with no tolerance for disrespectful or disruptive behavior. If behavior stayed above the line of disrespect, issues such as harassment, discrimination, or worse would never occur.

Even in the best of organizations—those with strong and positive cultures—disruptive behaviors do occur. When they do, they affect working relationships. If disruptive behaviors are not addressed, they can spiral down a slippery slope and erode into bigger problems.

➡ Appendix: Spiral of Disrespect

Deconstructing Disrespect

Disrespect is one of those words that can mean different things to different people. Like harassment, it's often used when people are in conflict with each other. Employees may invoke the words harassment or bullying when, in fact, neither exist.

Jarrod is asked to update the department's database. This specific task is not in his job descriptions; it's someone else's responsibility. So he protests and refuses to do it. After a heated exchange with his newly hired supervisor, he escalates his complaint to the department manager, saying that "the new guy" is treating him disrespectfully. After receiving a written reprimand for insubordination, he claims harassment because he spoke up for his rights (not to do a newly assigned task). This is not an example of harassment. Jarrod may not like being asked to do this new task. He may not like his supervisor speaking to him in a tone that is less than warm or friendly. Although Jarrod may *feel* like he's being harassed because he's being asked to do something new, there's no basis for a legal claim of harassment.

➡ Appendix: Employment Discrimination Laws and Related Websites

Three months later when it's time for Jarrod's performance review, both his supervisor, Frank, and the department manager, Brian, meet with him. Jarrod is not happy with their feedback or with the plan for improving his work performance, which had slipped along with his behavior. He raises his voice, uses course language, refuses to acknowledge the performance improvement plan, and storms out, heading to human resources to claim that he was being bullied. However, neither discipline for workplace behavior nor negative performance feedback with requests for improvement is an act of bullying.

Let's consider the following definitions as we explore different types of disrespectful behaviors:

* **Micro-inequities** can be looks, gestures, inflections, or body language of a dismissive nature. They are subtle and may or may not be intentional or isolated incidents. They can be rooted in stereotypes.

* **Discrimination** occurs in the workplace when decisions are made or a person receives unfair differential treatment based on a particular characteristic. When the characteristic

is protected by law, such as race or sex, the discrimination is illegal.

✳ **Harassment** is unwelcome conduct based on a particular characteristic, which may or may not be protected by law. If the behavior is based on a protected characteristic, it becomes unlawful when enduring the offensive conduct becomes a condition of continued employment; or the conduct is severe or pervasive enough to create a work environment that a reasonable person would consider intimidating, hostile, or abusive.[1]

✳ **Bullying** is the repeated infliction of intentional, malicious, and abusive behavior that interferes with a person's ability to do his/her work and is substantial enough to cause physical and/or psychological harm that a reasonable person would find it hostile or offensive.[2]

✳ **Workplace violence** is any act or threat of aggression that implicates the safety, security, or well-being of an individual who is at work.[3]

There is a relationship among all of these behaviors—atmosphere and working conditions—and the lines between them can be very thin.

Examining Micro-Inequities

The term "micro-inequities" was coined by MIT researcher Mary Rowe, PhD. They can include things like a weak handshake with little or no eye contact, listening with arms crossed, and looking at your watch, cell phone, or other device during presentations or while speaking with someone (unless you've been invited to do so). They have the effect of devaluing other individuals and negatively impacting feelings of inclusion and self-esteem. Employees, who feel devalued or excluded disengage and their contribution is diminished.[4]

Remember Jacob from Chapter 4? He was hovering over Claire while she was on a client call, sending a message that he was unhappy that Claire didn't put the call on hold. His behavior could be interpreted as controlling or menacing in some way—a more extreme, not-so-subtle micro-inequity.

> Drop the cutting sarcasm and thoughtless humor. Think of the message that's sent in this example: "Well, look who just arrived. Forget how to find the meeting room, did you?" Though this remark may be clever enough for a laugh, it's pointed enough to be nasty.[5]

Lori is one of two women on a team. She's rather soft-spoken compared to George, who is very aggressive and makes sure his opinions are heard. He's impatient with Lori's thoughtful approach and will often roll his eyes or make snarky comments when she speaks, such as "Did you say something?" implying she has nothing to contribute. Pete, the project manager, tends to ignore George's behavior because the two have many common interests. Several months into the project, Pete also starts ignoring Lori. Last week, Lori offered a technical solution to a vexing problem. Pete appeared not to be listening. When George offered the same solution, Pete responded with "Great idea, George." Besides monumental bad judgment, is Pete guilty of anything more than a micro-inequity behavior at this point? Probably not yet.

What if Pete acted on George's great idea and assigned him to lead a task force to address this vexing issue, passing Lori over for a developmental opportunity? The treatment is unfair to Lori. Pete's behavior *could be* moving closer to discrimination.

Is This Harassment?

Workplace harassment, sexual or otherwise, can take many forms, including:

* Jokes or comments of a sexual nature or that disparage specific groups such as ethnic groups;

* Graphic images;

* Gestures or lewd actions;

* Introduction of inappropriate topics, such as those of a sexual or racial nature into business conversations;

* Unwelcome hugging, touching, or other physical contact; or,

* Specific comments about someone's body or physical characteristics.

Joey likes to tell jokes and keep everyone's spirits high at work. His jokes are lighthearted and never mean-spirited. When he spots Penny in the break room looking a bit down, he tells her a silly joke he heard about surfer dudes and blonds (Joey's hair happens to blond). Penny smiles and laughs. Sally overhears this and gets upset, telling Joey that he's perpetrating the "dumb blond" stereotype and creating a hostile work environment toward women. (The surfer dudes were the brunt of the joke.) At worst, Joey may have been guilty of a micro-inequity, but the joke was neither severe nor pervasive enough that it would fit the definition of hostile work environment harassment.

Wendy had just joined the firm and found it odd when she began receiving e-mails with jokes and funny stories. When she asks about it, she's told, "We just try to keep things lively around here." There is nothing wrong with that; fun at work can be important. With time, however, the nature of the jokes begins to change, often becoming sexually suggestive or racially or ethnically pointed. Wendy finds them offensive and intimidating, making her uncomfortable. The behavior had eroded into hostile work environment harassment.

Before a meeting, Gene rolled his chair closer to Daria to look at her earrings, commenting they looked nice. She told him they'd been a gift from her boyfriend for her birthday. Later, he came into her office, pulled a chair very close, and told her she smelled nice and that her perfume was intriguing. Now she was growing uncomfortable. The next day he approached her and placed his hand on her shoulder, squeezed it firmly. Come to think of it, she'd seen him do this with other women: pay them compliments, then slowly move to behavior that was more personal and intimate. Clearly, Gene is exhibiting a pattern of unwelcome and unwanted behavior, in this case behavior of a sexual nature that is pervasive.

➡ Appendix: Preventing Harassment—
Managers' Guide
➡ Appendix: Workplace Harassment—
Employee Rights and Responsibilities

Where's the Bully?

Like harassment, workplace bullying can take many forms, including shouting, screaming, or other verbal abuse; singling someone out for unjustified criticism or blame; excluding someone from work activities; purposefully ignoring work contributions; using language or actions that embarrass or humiliate; or, making jokes that repeatedly target the same person.[6]

Remember Renata from Chapter 9? Her behavior went beyond interrupting and making snide comments. Left unchecked, she could be especially aggressive. When confronting Mark with her accusations, she slammed a file onto his desk as she leaned forward and pounded her fist. Was she merely making sure that she, unlike Lori, was heard when she talked, or had she crossed that thin line and now was walking the path to becoming a bully?

Meanwhile, Wendy received an e-mail one morning that was likely poking fun at Ian, a coworker. She could tell from the subject line it was yet another joke and she deleted it. Even more disturbing was when other associates started responding with seemingly mean-spirited comments. When she asked what was going on, Nicola responded, "We're just having some harmless fun at Ian's expense. After all, he can be difficult at times!" When workplace fun is targeted toward one individual or group of individuals, when it is one way and the targeted individual is not participating, and when it's personal, such as comments about someone's body type, it can quickly erode beyond disrespectful. In this case, the comments were cruel and many people were participating. The behavior was eroding and, if not addressed soon, was in danger of slipping to the level of bullying.

> Many believe that bullying is the younger sibling to violence. Recognize that there's a relationship between verbal aggression (such as harassment and bullying) and actual physical violence. Disruptive behaviors should not be seen as completely separate, but rather as part of an environmental ailment that weakens the organizational immune system and allows violence in.[7]

When Lars joined the organization, he was enthusiastically welcomed. Accomplished in his profession, he brought a great deal of expertise. His relationship with his peers and Lorraine, his manager, started positively. Just as he was getting comfortable in his new role, Lorraine's attitude started to change. At first, she'd respond to his input in staff meetings with snarky comments and sarcasm, sometimes even belittling his work or his credentials. Then she started excluding Lars from meetings and, if questioned, responded that his presence wasn't necessary. However, when he didn't complete assignments that were discussed in the meetings—assignments about which he had no knowledge—she'd yell at him publicly, scathingly attacking his work and tossing humiliating insults. As if that wasn't enough, she started making sly comments about him online. Others were quite surprised by her behavior and morale began to decline. Lorraine had realized that Lars's qualifications and background far exceeded hers. She was intentionally being abusive, and she was creating a toxic work environment for everyone.

As Frank and Brian struggle to align changes in the department to those in their industry, Jarrod continues to challenge Frank. He questions him constantly about what process to follow, what changes will be made next, or how he should interact with Frank on assignments. He badgers Frank with e-mails, often as many as 25 per day. His questions and comments are filled with offensive language and are often accompanied by insults and shouts. Because of Jarrod's physical size and temperament, Frank is intimidated by both his presence and behavior. When Frank loses his composure and shouts back, Jarrod accuses him of bullying, when, in fact, he is the one engaging in the bully behavior.

Establish Boundaries

Boundaries have eroded as today's workplaces have become more relaxed and informal. Yet boundaries—those invisible lines that help define roles and manage interpersonal relationships at work—are important. Boundaries define limits—where you end and where others begin. They define responsibilities and foster accountability. Gene clearly crossed a physical boundary with Daria. Boundaries also define limits for language and communication. They are a close cousin to expectations.

➡ Chapter 6: You Want Me to Do What?

Watch your language when sharing public space with others. Be mindful that other people of varying demographics may have different values and standards. Be courteous. Keep your voice down. Use cell phones with discretion. Avoid explicit or intimate conversations.

Choose a neutral vocabulary that minimizes the possibility of offending, angering, or embarrassing those within earshot.[8]

Even in non-hierarchical organizations, boundaries at work establish clarity for job responsibilities and relationships such as who is responsible for giving job assignments and feedback. The reprimand that Jarrod received stated that his job description includes a provision for other related duties as assigned. It reiterated established responsibilities and relationships. The boundaries were clear.

Establishing boundaries also helps to differentiate between issues in our personal lives versus those in our professional lives. Maintaining a balance between openness and privacy, even in an era where social media is so prevalent, is important. Look at the difference between the following two statements:

✳ "I just moved to the area." (Open statement.)

✳ "I just moved to the area and my spouse and I fight now fight constantly." (Private statement.)

Play it safe. Topics best avoided in workplace conversations include:[9]

✳ Detailed health problems,

✳ Details of sex life or sexual activity,

✳ Problems with spouse, partner, or family member,

✳ Personal finances (positive or negative),

> * Personal religious views,
> * Political topics that evoke passion, and
> * Gossip or discussions about coworkers' personal lives.

If you're the recipient of too much information, be polite and non-judgmental as you let it be known that the information makes you uncomfortable or is not an appropriate topic for work. You can use phrases such as:

* "I'm not comfortable talking about... [for example, personal issues]."
* "I don't think this is an appropriate topic to be discussing at work."
* "I don't appreciate... [for example, that type of humor, those remarks or comments]."

Intent vs. Impact

Wendy's colleagues started out to have fun. Did it matter that they didn't mean for their behavior to be offensive or intimidating? Regarding sexual harassment, most courts have generally held that the effect of the conduct on the person who is on the receiving end determines if the conduct constitutes sexual harassment. The underlying premise comes from the reasonable-person standard. Would a reasonable person consider the conduct harassing, intimidating, and/or offensive? Men and women generally hold differing perspectives about behavior that could be sexual harassment. Thus, the courts have held that harassing conduct must be evaluated from the perspective of the victim.[10]

> People are affected by different things, differ-
> ent jokes, and different language. A joke you
> tell within your circle of friends and family may
> not be offensive to them, but you can't assume
> that it won't be offensive to someone at work.
> You may intend to be lighthearted, but if the
> subject touches on protected characteristics,
> for example, someone may conclude that your
> behavior is harassment.

That's the legal standard for determining unlawful harassment. Though not all disruptive behavior is harassment, it's a good standard to use. In workplace conflicts, we may be tempted to assume the other person's intentions from the impact their behavior has on us. We feel hurt, slighted, or dismissed—micro-inequities. We can't know what their intentions are because they exist only with the other person.[11]

Equally important, we can't assume that despite our intention, our behavior won't have a negative impact on others. We don't know what other people's sensitivities are. Ian may have been teased by older siblings as a child and the comments in the e-mails may bring back some painful memories.

Tatiana had an abusive stepfather with a fierce temper. He would often grab her arm, just to get her attention. As a result, she developed a very low tolerance for anyone touching her. Her coworker Roland had quirky mannerisms that included touching people on the arm or shoulder when he talked to them, which made many people uncomfortable. However, Roland didn't seem to pick up on the signals people were sending. One day, in an attempt to get her attention, he grabbed Tatiana's arm. She reacted and took a swing at him while her coffee cup was still in her hand, causing quite a scene as a shouting match between the two followed.

To avoid conflict, try to disentangle impact from intent. To frame your discussion with the other person, ask yourself three questions:

1. Actions: "What did the other person actually say or do?"

2. Impact: "What was the impact of this on me?"

3. Assumptions: "Based on this impact, what assumptions am I making about what the other person intended?"[12]

Priya and Jon are colleagues. During lunch one day, Jon leans over and tells her that he finds her exotic looks very sensual. Just then, the waitress returns with their change and Priya hurriedly grabs her things and says, "Time to get back to work."

Later, Priya asks herself the three questions. Now she has a starting point for her conversation with Jon, which begins as follows: "Jon, I was surprised you made that comment at lunch. It was uncharacteristic of you and made me feel embarrassed. I could have assumed you did it purposefully so I'd be thrown off guard in the meetings we have to attend together." Priya didn't make any accusations. She related what he did and said (he can't refute he made the statement), explained its impact on her, and stated *her* assumption of his intention. This gave Jon the opportunity to explain his actions in a non-threatening way.

Respectful Confrontations

There are many things that may motivate someone to behave in a disruptive manner. Is it narcissism (perhaps George or Jarrod?), low self-confidence (perhaps Lorraine?), or low emotional intelligence—just plain cluelessness (perhaps Roland?); or, an environment that turns a blind eye to such behavior (perhaps Wendy's or Lori's situation?). Just like with intent, it's futile to try to figure out why. It's more effective to determine the best approach to confront the situation and resolve the conflict.

Say "no" to a request or demand that is unwelcome, a behavior that is inappropriate or abusive, or a situation that is not fair. However, you also must make it clear that the behavior has to change:

* Describe the disruptive behavior.
* Explain the impact it had on you or others.
* Ask for the behavior to stop.

After giving Jon the opportunity to explain, Priya needs to ask that he stop making personal comments. Wendy went along with the jokes from her coworkers until they reached the point of becoming offensive to her. She can explain that though the initial jokes were fine, the ones that are of a sexual, ethnic, or racial nature are not okay, that they make her uncomfortable, and to please remove her from the e-mail list. She's not attacking the individuals sending the e-mails, but she is pointing out their behavior. In this case, because workplace harassment is involved, management intervention should take place.

If you're receiving a respectful confrontation:

❋ Listen, with full attention.

❋ Don't get defensive.

❋ Remember intent vs. impact.

❋ Ask for specifics. "Help me understand how I violated a boundary."

❋ Express gratitude for bringing the matter to your attention.

❋ Apologize, if appropriate.

When Gene admired Daria's earrings, he seemingly was making an innocent comment. When he remarked about her perfume, he crossed a thin line. Daria could have sent a direct but neutral message that the behavior was not appropriate: "It's okay to offer a compliment or admire a piece of jewelry. It's not okay to get close and comment on my perfume or scent. That behavior is creepy. Please don't do it again. If you want to have a conversation, please honor my personal space and don't get so close when you speak to me."

When Lorraine began disparaging Lars's work in meetings, he could have let her know that the comments were not okay with him: "Please stop! I can take criticism, but putting me down in front of other people is embarrassing for me, for you, and for everyone present. If you have issues with my work, let's talk privately."

When Ian became aware of the e-mails being sent with taunting comments about him, he could have confronted Nicola, who started the e-mail chain, in a firm yet polite manner: "Please stop teasing me. It's disruptive and it humiliates both of us. If you have work issues with me, come and talk to me directly, but please don't try to have fun at my expense."

Roland's behavior caught Tatiana by surprise and rather than think, she reacted. It's unfortunate that no one said anything to him about his annoying mannerisms before the altercation. Once things calmed down, Tatiana explained her reaction: "Look, it's not okay to grab me. You're strong and you had a firm grip on my arm. Your actions were physically intimidating. Please refrain from touching or grabbing me in the future. If you want to get my attention, say something or send me a text or e-mail."

All of these examples sent a strong, firm, yet polite message about the behavior, not the person. They were clear, feasible, positively framed, and respectful. All described the behavior and its impact and asked that it stop. All offered an alternative to the behavior—a constructive way that the relationships can continue in a manner where everyone feels respected. When all else fails, bring it back to respect.

Essential Tips

   ✻   If relationships become damaged, they have to be fixed because they affect the entire workplace and the organization.

   ✻   When in doubt, think about the impact that your behavior may have on others.

   ✻   Employment discrimination laws don't guarantee a utopian work environment or protect employees from personality or workplace conflict.

* When dealing with disruptive behavior, don't accommodate, don't avoid, and don't attack.

* Be hard on the problem and the behavior, but not on the person.

CHAPTER 11

WHAT'S AN ORGANIZATION TO DO?

The harder the conflict, the more glorious the triumph.

—Thomas Paine

Even if you don't think so, you do have options to help you and your organization address serious workplace conflict and behavior issues. All is not lost! In this chapter, we're going to explore some of what is available to managers and organizations to make it a little easier to handle difficult situations when they come up—and they will. We're going to look at:

* Good management techniques.
* Management training options.
* Policies that can help:
    o Conflict resolution.
    o Harassment.
    o Bullying.
* Wellness programs.
* Employee Assistance Programs.
* Employee training options.
* Flexible work schedules.
* Alternative dispute resolution, including peer review panels.

You're probably familiar with defining management as "getting things done through others." This sounds easy enough, so why is it so incredibly difficult to successfully manage people today? Good managers understand that their real job is to inspire their employees to do their absolutely best work and to create a work environment where good work can be accomplished.

We've talked a lot in previous chapters about good communication skills and establishing trust in the workplace; these are two incredibly important skills and much needed to be a successful manager. They are critical when establishing a culture where conflict is encouraged and effectively managed in order to move the organization forward (see chapters 1 and 5).

Management Techniques

In order to create a culture where conflict is encouraged and effectively managed, managers have to

be approachable. Remember the old "open-door" policy that we used to talk about? That was back in the day
when managers had doors on their offices. Today, many
organizations have gone to open-floor concepts where
everyone works in cubicles or, if managers and people
above them have offices, they may not have doors. So,
the term "open door" should not be taken literally; just
think of it as managers needing to be available to their
people.

Consider this situation: A team has been meeting
for three weeks on a project they've been told is of great
importance to their organization. They've reached an
impasse and need their manager to help them take the
next step. At the end of the meeting, the team leader
stops by the manager's desk, but she's not there. He e-
mails the manager and asks for 10 minutes by the end
of the day. Two hours later he gets a text that says she's
tied up in a budget meeting that will go into the eve-
ning and she's off on a business trip the next day. Can
they talk next week? The team leader goes back to the
team to tell them they probably aren't going to get with
the manager today and maybe not for a while, so they
try to move ahead. Because they don't have what they
need, conflicts come up and the project is stalled.

Of course, everyone is busy, but being accessible to
your employees is a management imperative and, in
today's 24/7 world, we all stay connected all the time.
Maybe this manager could have stepped out of the
budget meeting for a quick 10 minutes with her team
leader and then the group could have continued to
make progress as opposed to being stuck until she was
free. Think open door—even when there aren't actual
doors!

Another potential source of workplace conflict is unclear expectations. Managers must be clear with associates as to what is expected of them and in what time frame. Has this ever happened to you? Your manager quickly outlines something he/she wants you to do and sends you on your way. You get right to it and return with the finished project and hear, "That's not what I wanted." Or, you get a call from the manager at the end of the morning asking when you will be finished and you thought you had a week to get it done! Clear expectations are critical to good working relationships and for avoiding the kind of conflict that is disruptive and hostile. A good manager is clear when setting expectations and is also open to having employees ask questions like "When do you need this?" or "Can I come back to you if I have a question as I work on this?" And, think about how much better it is when employees know what is expected of them and have clear access to their manager when needed.

➡ Chapter 6: You Want Me to Do What?

Management Training

I used to work with a high-level executive who said that you can't teach people to manage others; it is a skill you are born with. Well, I totally disagree with that! I think you can certainly train people in the very skills they need to be an effective manager. Here are some of the most important training opportunities a well-managed organization should offer to anyone *before* they take on managerial responsibilities, and this list is certainly not all-inclusive:

✳ Communication skills (listening, speaking, business writing, and presentation skills).

✳ Conflict management skills.

✳ Critical conversation skills.

✳ Harassment prevention skills.

✳ Diversity and inclusion skills.

✳ Delegation skills.

✳ Counseling skills.

✳ Coaching skills.

✳ Mentoring skills.

✳ Interviewing skills.

✳ Performance management skills (feedback, goal setting, and performance appraisal skills).

✳ Conducting an effective meeting.

✳ Team-building skills.

✳ Change management skills.

✳ Effective use of technology.

As Mitchell and Gamlem write in *The Big Book of HR*, there are many ways that training can be delivered, including in-house programs, public workshops/seminars, online training, programs at local universities, or corporate universities.[1]

Mentoring can also be a very cost-effective way to develop new managers. Use your existing great managers to mentor employees who are being promoted into a managerial role.

Policies

Having well-written policies can be very helpful in conflict management situations. For example, if your firm has a policy of how conflicts should be handled in your organization, and everyone who joins the organization is trained on the policy and how to use it, people have a place to start when trouble happens. I wish I could say that if you have a conflict resolution policy, conflict will go away, but that's not going to happen. You still employ people and people have conflicts.

If your organization determines it is advisable to have a conflict resolution policy, it should include:

* Purpose of the policy.
* Eligibility to bring claims.
* How to file a claim and with whom.
* Time frame to file a claim from date of precipitating incident (if applicable).
* Action to be taken if the situation isn't resolved.
* Process for appeal, if any.
* Time frame for appeals, if any.
* Who should be involved in the resolution (HR, outside mediator, labor attorney, etc.).
* Non-retaliation policy.

➡ Appendix: Sample Conflict Resolution Policy

Policies also serve the purpose of helping organizations to set expectations. Organizations often develop policies that address performance and workplace conduct. A performance management policy should:

✳ Provide a process for managers to communicate job expectations and to formally evaluate performance against those expectations.

✳ Describe clear expectations that must be related to job performance such as skills, behaviors, and tasks important for job success, and should be:

  ○ Specific, measurable, and observable.

  ○ Within the employee's control.

  ○ Achievable with time and resources.

✳ Encourage informal evaluation and communication on a continual basis.

✳ Develop a culture of continued improvement.

✳ Require communication of performance expectations.

✳ Provide a process for performance improvement to correct performance below expectations.

✳ Provide a process for continued performance success for "star" performers.[2]

A workplace conduct policy should:

✳ Establish and define professional standards of conduct that are not acceptable, while stressing that the list is not all inclusive and that there can be other infractions.

✳ Provide assistance to employees to change inappropriate behavior.

✳ Provide management a means to address issues.

* Provide management responses if behavior does not change.

* Provide a flexible approach (progressive or corrective discipline) process to address conduct.

* Provide communication mechanisms for employees and managers.

A corrective discipline process can include these steps:

* Open dialogue/verbal counseling.

* Written counseling/letter of caution.

* Final written notice.

* Suspension.

* Termination.

A fair and defensible corrective discipline process allows management flexibility in determining whether all steps should be used in dealing with a specific problem and in deciding when immediate or severe action must be taken. Don't be too specific in your process and tie management's hands. Disciplinary action can and should start at any stage depending on the severity of the behavior. Don't factor judgment out of the process.[3]

Organizations should also have a harassment policy that is communicated to all employees and in writing. The policy should cover all forms of harassment, not just sexual harassment, and provide:

* A definition of harassment with clear explanations of prohibited conduct.

* A definition of the responsibilities of all employees, the responsibilities of management

employees, and the responsibilities of human resources.

❋ Assurance against retaliation.

❋ A clear complaint process.

❋ Assurance of confidentiality to the extent possible.

❋ A clear investigation process.

❋ Assurance of corrective action when harassment has occurred.[4]

Finally, the organization should have a policy that prohibits discrimination that applies to employees and applicants and that ensures that all employee practices are administered without unlawful discrimination on any protected basis.[5]

Workplace Bullying

It has become more common for bullying to happen in the workplace. Bullying can take a variety of forms, but it is commonly defined as repeated, health-harming mistreatment of one or more persons (the targets) by one or more perpetrators. It is abusive conduct that is threatening, humiliating, or intimidating; or is work interference (sabotage), which prevents work from getting done or, is verbal abuse.

Bullying can cause emotional stress and has a ripple effect within organizations because bullies breed other bullies if left unchecked.

Bullies can be managers or employees or coworkers, and organizations have to be vigilant in order to stop bullying behavior as quickly as possible. Consider that employees can bully managers as easily as the other way around.

Organizations should develop, implement, and communicate a bullying policy. This policy should be included in your employee handbook and discussed with all new hires during the on-boarding process. It is also a good idea to discuss this policy (and others) from time to time in all-staff meetings or in employee newsletters to keep the concepts fresh in the minds of your staff. Included in the policy should be:

* Objective (purpose of the policy).

* Who it covers (all employees, management, executives, etc.).

* Definition of workplace bullying.

* Examples of behaviors that will not be tolerated.

* How to report workplace bullying.

* Investigation process when workplace bullying is reported.

* Consequences of workplace behavior (action that will be taken).

➡ Chapter 10: Are You Playing Nice in the Sandbox?

Wellness Programs

Many organizations now have wellness programs that can be helpful in creating a culture where conflict is rare, and when it arises, it moves the organization forward as opposed to stopping it cold. These programs yield healthier and more productive employees and can help reduce the stress related to working in today's increasingly complex environments. Many wellness programs also include family members of employees and may include nutrition programs, weight loss, smoking cessation, stress-reduction techniques (including yoga), mindfulness, and fitness programs.[6]

As Scott Eblin says in *Overworked and Overwhelmed*, "Does it feel like it's gotten worse over the past several years? Most of the people I talk to and work with feel like it feels crazier lately."[7] He goes on to talk about all the technology advances we've made in the past few years including the smart phone. Has the smartphone helped or hurt us? Yes, we all now carry a powerful computer in our pocket that takes great pictures and allows us to play games when we're standing in line, but what else has it done? Eblin says, "A survey of executives, managers, and professionals conducted by the Center for Creative Leadership in 2013 shows that the typical smartphone carrying executive, manager, and professional is interacting with work an average of 72 hours a week." He continues that at that pace of work—after you subtract time for eating, sleeping, and personal hygiene—we end up with only about 40 hours a week for everything else we want or need to do. Is it any wonder people feel stressed?

One way of dealing with the issues of today's complex world is a stress-reduction technique called mindfulness. Jon Kabat-Zinn created the Mindfulness-Based Stress Reduction Program at the University of Massachusetts Medical Center in 1979 and now more than 200 hospitals around the world have adopted similar programs. Eblin quotes Kabat-Zinn's definition of mindfulness as "the awareness that arises by paying attention on purpose in the present moment and nonjudgmentally."[8] Your Employee Assistance Program may offer mindfulness training, which can be a valuable resource as you work to help your employees deal with stress and manage workplace conflicts.

Employee Assistance Programs (EAP)

One of the best tools available to organizations and to managers is your Employee Assistance Program. EAPs can help employees identify and resolve concerns related to health, marital situations, family, finances, substance abuse, legal matters, emotional problems, stress, workplace violence, bullying, or other personal issues that can impact job performance. They can be in-house programs or offered through an outside contractor.[9] EAP professionals can be extremely helpful when workplace conflicts are related to stress. Many EAPs also offer mediation services to their clients.

Examples of Referrals to an EAP

Access to EAP services are typically through a referral. Common types of referrals include:

* Self-referrals, where an employee voluntarily seeks assistance for an issue affecting his/her life, either at work or away from work.

* Management referrals, which are voluntary referrals based on tangible, observed, and documented indicators of deteriorating job performance or behavior. If an employee fails to take advantage of the EAP, no direct management action should be taken, but the organization should continue to hold the employee accountable for performance and conduct,

and take appropriate action if there is further deterioration.

✳ Mandatory referrals generally occur as the result of a positive drug test or when violent or potentially violent behavior is exhibited. Unlike management referrals, employees can be subject to management action, including termination for failure to contact the EAP. Employees are often placed on leave until they contact the EAP, comply with a course of treatment, and receive an appropriate fitness-for-duty report.

We suggest that managers be trained on how to use the EAP. EAPs are a tremendous resource when used appropriately and can help with conflict management situations when needed.

Employee Training

Today's workers are hungry for development and training. Savvy organizations offer training in a variety of topics to all employees, not just management or leadership level staff. Consider offering to all levels of the organization a subset of the training that is provided to your managers; just tailor the content to their jobs and eliminate the parts of the programs that focus on managerial skill development.

Consider how effective it might be for your employees to take conflict management training so that they learn techniques to avoid some of the negative impacts of unresolved conflict.

Workplace Flexibility

Increasingly, employees are looking for ways to make their lives simpler, and one of the most valued benefits today is being able to have some flexibility in scheduling work. As Mitchell and Gamlem say in *The Big Book of HR*, "A workplace environment that allows employees to change when and how they work, based on their needs and job responsibilities, relieves work/life conflict and reduces turnover, according to a study by the University of Minnesota."[10]

Workplace flexibility takes many forms, including:

* Part-time or reduced-hours schedules.

* Telecommuting from a satellite location, or working from home on specific days or full-time.

* Flex-time with core hours where employees choose their start- and end-times, but must be present during specific times of the day.

* A compressed work week where full-time employees work longer days for part of the week or pay period in exchange for shorter days or an additional day off each week or pay period.

There are many other options for organizations that want to relieve employee stress and, perhaps, reduce workplace conflict situations, but it is important to have policies in place that meet the needs of your workforce. It is also critical that programs be fair and equitable, and that managers are trained in how to manage remote employees, if applicable. Also, be sure your programs comply with the Fair Labor Standards Act (FLSA), the Family and Medical Leave Act (FMLA), the Occupational Safety and Health Act (OSHA), and any other applicable laws.

Alternative Dispute Resolution Methods

Alternative dispute resolution (ADR) is a problem-solving technique that generally uses a trained, third-party neutral panel.

In Chapter 9, we talked about a manager or HR professional assuming the role of mediator to help solve conflicts. In addition, organizations can use external mediators. Mediation is a method of dispute resolution that uses a neutral third party to facilitate communication between individuals to promote a resolution based on the individuals' interests. Traditionally, trained mediators who do not work for the organization have been used. However, employees can be trained to serve as mediators and some organizations are implementing formal peer mediation programs. A mediator does not have decision-making authority but acts as a facilitator and helps the individuals involved in the dispute to come to a mutually acceptable agreement.

Peer review panels can be an effective way for organizations to resolve workplace conflicts. The peer review process uses a group of managers and employees who are trained in the organization's policies and are empowered to make final decisions on a specific range of work-related issues. Unlike a mediator, the peer review panel has the authority to render a decision that is binding on the people involved. Time and costs are involved for training panel members as well as the time and labor costs spent participating on the panel.

Employees serving on peer review panels have the opportunity to interact with managers to reach a fair decision, and they become messengers for management's genuine concern about doing the right thing and creating a positive work environment.

The American Arbitration Association (AAA) is a public-service, not-for-profit organization that offers a broad range of dispute resolution services to organizations around the country. Hearings may be held at locations convenient for the organizations involved and are not limited to cities with AAA offices. In addition, the Federal Mediation and Conciliation Service provides mediation services.

Workplace conflict is a fact of life, but you have many resources available to you to help you manage those conflicts effectively. We hope this book will provide you with what you need to successfully navigate the world of workplace conflict and we've also provided you with a bibliography for additional help if needed!

Essential Tips

* No matter how good a manager you are, there will be conflicts in your organization.
* Train your managers to handle conflict.
* Have well-written and well-communicated policies including on conflict resolution and bullying.
* Consider adding a wellness program.
* Make good use of your Employee Assistance Program.
* Train your employees to handle conflict.

✳ Allow as much flexibility as your work permits.

✳ Use alternative dispute resolution methods if needed, including peer review panels.

AFTERWORD

Whenever two or more people come together to live, play, or work, there are going to be differences. In the best of situations, there'll be creativity; in the worst, there'll be conflict.

In *The Essential Workplace Conflict Handbook*, we presented a variety of situations in which people at work were in conflict. Through these examples, we tried to help our readers understand why these conflicts might exist. Our intent was to provide tips and insights into managing conflict in your workplace. However, conflict is complicated and often complex. Each encounter has to be acknowledged, assessed, and addressed on its own circumstances and merits. Managing conflict takes time, patience, and practice. It doesn't come easily for many people and there's an art to perfecting conflict resolution. The next time you encounter it, go to the balcony, take a deep breath, and thumb through this book again.

After we finished writing *The Big Book of HR*, we jokingly told people, "We're still talking to each other!" We recognize that our working styles are different, but we don't let our differences interfere with our work. We don't have time for interferences. We've got more books to write!

Cornelia Gamlem

Barbara Mitchell

Washington, D.C.

ADDITIONAL RESOURCES

Seven Dimensions of Culture

(The following table on pages 206, 207, and 208 is based on the model developed by Fons Trompenaars and Charles Hampden-Turner as published in their book, *Riding the Waves of Culture*.)

Rules vs. Relationships

Universalism		Particularism
• High importance on laws, rules, values and obligations. • Deal fairly, but rules come before relationships.		• Each circumstance and each relationship dictates the rules they live by. • Responses to a situation may change based on specific facts, events, and people.

The Individual vs. The Group

Individualism		Communitarianism
• Rewards, credit, and responsibility assigned to individuals. • Make decisions and care for self. • Individual accomplishment and initiative prized.		• Shared responsibility and accountability. • Group is more important than the individual. • Individual accomplishments and initiative discouraged, downplayed.

How Far People Get Involved

Specific		Diffuse
• Separate work from personal lives. • Don't see relationships having an impact on work objectives.		• Overlap between work and personal lives. • Good relationships are vital to business objectives.

How People Express Emotions

Neutral		Emotional
• Make effort to control emotions. • Reason influences actions more than feelings. • Don't reveal what they are thinking or feeling.		• Look for ways to express emotions, even spontaneously. • Expressing emotions is welcome and accepted.

How People View Status

Achievement		Ascription
• You are what you do. • Your worth is based on what you do. • Performance is valued no matter who you are.		• Value lies in who you are. • Power, title, and position matter. • Roles define behavior.

How People Manage Time

Sequential Time		Synchronous Time
• Events happen in order. • Priority on promptness, staying on schedule and deadlines. • Time is money.		• Past, present, and future are interwoven periods. • Work on several projects at once. • Plans and commitments are flexible.

How People Relate to Their Environment

Internal Direction (or internal locus of control)		Outer Direction (or external locus of control)
• Belief that nature and environment can be controlled to achieve goals. • This belief extends to how they work with teams within the organization.		• Belief that nature and the environment control them and they must work within their environment to achieve goals. • Focus their actions on others and avoid conflict when possible.

Barriers to Communication

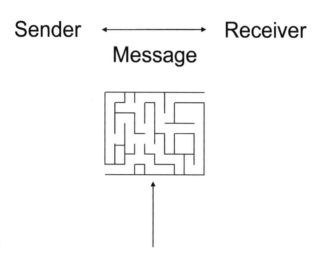

Sender ⟷ Receiver

Message

Culture, Gender, Age, Education, Work Experience,
Communication Style, Geography, Approach to Change,
Problem-Solving Style, Approach to Conflict, etc.

Diversity Self-Assessment Planner

1. **Examine your first response to someone who is different.**

2. **Review your specific assumptions about the person.**

4. **Find commonalities and build trust.**

3. **Check the reality behind your assumptions.**

Examples of Team Conflicts

Any of these can result in team members being in conflict with other team members.

* Unclear team purpose—why are we together and what are we expected to accomplish?

* Unclear roles on the team. For example, who is the team leader?

* Poor choice of a team leader.

* Unproductive team meetings.

* Disruptive behavior that is unresolved.

* Lack of cooperation between team members.

* Diversity issues (see Chapter 2).

* Withholding information from other members of the team.

* Lack of interest/commitment.

* Cliques within the team.

* Frequent changes in direction.

* Unrealistic expectations.

* Lack of support from outside the team.

* Team members not pulling their weight and expecting others to pick up the slack.

* Personality conflicts between team members.

* Not having the tools to accomplish the team goals.

Working With Emotions

Emotions affect how you see a problem, how the other person sees a problem, and in many cases may be a big part of what is wrong.

✳   Be aware of emotions—yours and theirs—when they arise. Have you done something that humiliated them? Are they disappointed with your suggestions for how to handle a problem? Do they feel you are ignoring them?

✳   Find the cause of the emotion(s). Is anger related to the current problem or something that happened a long time ago? Is it something still worth being upset about? Are you frustrated with yourself because you didn't do something you were supposed to do? Is your boss mad at you because his boss is mad at him?

✳   Don't place blame. It's never productive and focuses on the past, making everyone, including yourself, feel bad. It accomplishes nothing.

✳   Acknowledge and discuss emotions. You may want to ask what it is that makes the other person feel anxious, angry, etc. Say something such as: "It seems like you're upset about something. Maybe we should talk about what's making you upset before we continue." People can feel vulnerable when discussing emotions. By raising the subject, you are letting them know you care about them, are willing to listen, and that you too are vulnerable.

✳   You can't disagree with an emotion. Respect what others say about their emotions. They know how they feel better than you do. On the other hand, when you are conveying your emotions, say, "I felt hurt (angry, anxious, etc.) when you failed to (include me in the discussion, follow up on the assignment, etc.)."

Self-Reflection Exercise

What is your listening style?

Circle the responses that most closely reflect how you listen. You may use a different listening style in different situations.

Appreciative Listening

- ✳ Listen to enjoy the experience—motivated by enjoyment.

- ✳ Focus is to be entertained.

- ✳ Tune out when they are no longer interested. (Give someone a remote control and watch them switch the channel when they lose interest.)

- ✳ Appropriate when someone is telling a joke or good story, going to a concert, comedy club, or other fun activity.

Empathic Listening

- ✳ Listen to support the speaker.

- ✳ Focus is to show concern.

- ✳ Motivated by desire to impact the person talking by providing an opportunity to express their feelings ("a shoulder to cry on").

* Appropriate when counseling, allowing someone to blow off steam, or bonding with someone with whom you want/have a good relationship.

Comprehensive Listening

* Listen to organize the information being given by the speaker.

* Focus is to make sense out of the information.

* Motivated by a chance to apply what they are hearing to their own experience.

* Enjoy picking out the main idea and supporting ideas to help create an organized message.

* Appropriate when taking directions, helping someone make sense of scattered thoughts, or trying to determine an action to take.

Discerning Listening

* Listen to gather information.

* Focus is to get the complete picture and information.

* Motivated by the desire to find the main message and sort out details.

* Appropriate in learning situations where the goal is to gather as much information as possible.

* Usually have many questions.

Evaluative Listening

* Listening to move to action and fix the situation.

* Focus is on making a decision from the available information.

* Motivated to relate information to their personal beliefs and question motives behind the message in order to accept or reject the message and move to action or fix the problem.

* Appropriate when you need to make a decision, vote on something, draw conclusions, or move to fix something.

The Communication Cycle

Sender

Feedback
(Impact)

↗ ↘
↖ ↙

Message
(Intent)

Receiver

Position vs. Interest—An Exercise

Reflect on a past conflict you had in which what the other person wanted seemed to conflict with what you said you wanted. Use the following format to examine the positions and interests:

* ❊ Briefly describe the event.

* ❊ What was your stated position? What was it that you wanted?

* ❊ Why did you take this position? Why did you want it?

* ❊ What were you saying no to? What activity or behavior did you want to say yes to?

* ❊ What were you seeking to change? Why?

* ❊ What core value(s) were you seeking to protect? Why?

* ❊ To the best of your ability, why might they have wanted what they said they wanted? (Try to give them the benefit of the doubt rather than assuming negative motivations.)

* ❊ What were they saying no to? What activity or behavior might they want to say yes to?

* ❊ What might they have been seeking to change? Why?

* ❊ What core value(s) were they seeking to protect? Why?

Hersey/Blanchard Situational Leadership Model

Supporting or Participating	Coaching/Selling
Leaders pass day-to-day decisions, such as task allocation and process, to the follower. The leader facilitates and takes part in decisions, but control is with the follower.	Leaders still define roles and tasks, but seek ideas and suggestions from the follower. Decisions are the leader's prerogative, but communication is much more two-way.
Delegating	**Directing/Telling**
Leaders are still involved in decisions and problem solving, but control is with the follower. The follower is responsible for implementation and decides when and how the leader will be involved.	Leaders define the roles and tasks of the followers and supervise them closely. Decisions are made by the leader and announced to the followers. Communication is largely one-way.

Discovering Your Conflict Style
(adapted from *The Power of a Good Fight*)

Competing

1. Do you enjoy the give and take of a good argument?

2. Are you competitive—even in situations where the results aren't very important to you?

3. Do coworkers frequently give in to you because it's too much trouble to work things out?

4. Are there some people in the organization who avoid you or fear interaction with you?

If you answered yes to two or more of these questions, your preferred style is competing.

Accommodating

1. Is loyalty one of your highest values?

2. Is it important to you to have coworkers like you?

3. Do you give in during disagreements—even if you think you have a better idea—because you believe it's best for your team or organization?

4. Are you constantly trying to take care of the feelings of others or to make them feel better?

If you answered yes to two or more of these questions, your preferred style is accommodating.

Avoiding

1. Do you generally avoid conflict even when the issue is important to you?

2. Are you frequently unsure about where you stand on a particular issue that others seem to feel strongly about?

3. Do you avoid certain people in your organization who have abrasive or competitive styles?

4. Do you prefer to have time to think before you speak or answer questions?

If you answered yes to two or more of these questions, your preferred style is avoiding.

Compromising

1. When you're upset with a coworker, do you feel a need to talk to someone else about the issue?

2. Does the idea of confronting someone directly with your issues intimidate you?

3. Do others at your level of the organization come to you to talk about their problems with their coworkers?

4. Do you need to talk extensively about your feelings with someone before you're sure what you think and feel?

If you answered yes to two or more of these questions, your preferred style is compromising.

Collaborating

1.   Do others frequently ask you to mediate their disputes?

2.   Do you consistently step back from the emotion of a conflict and think before responding?

3.   Are you able to see the big picture during disagreements?

4.   Are you able to remember and consider your own goals as well as your organization's goals during an argument?

5.   Do others tell you that you are a good listener?

If you answered yes to two or more of these questions, your preferred style is collaborating.

Preparing to Mediate: A Checklist

If you're called upon to mediate a conflict, the questions presented in this checklist can help you organize your thoughts about the problem-solving process.

People

* ❋ How do they see the problem?
* ❋ Are emotions part of the problem?
* ❋ Are they having any misunderstandings?

Interests

* ❋ What are the interests of each person to the conflict?
* ❋ Can they each articulate their needs, wants, hopes, and fears?

Inventing Options

* ❋ Have the individuals focused on options?
* ❋ Have they tried brainstorming?

Fairness

* ❋ Has each person identified standards of fairness to help address the problem?
* ❋ Have fair procedures been identified?

Yourself

* ❋ Do I have the vantage point of a neutral observer?

* Can I describe the problem in a way that rings true for all involved?

* Do I understand that the individuals involved have to determine the solution?

Employment Discrimination Laws and Related Websites

This list is not meant to be all-inclusive. There are additional federal laws, as well as state and local laws, that impact working relationships. Laws and regulations are not static, and they frequently change. The resolution of each circumstance encountered by readers should ultimately be determined on a case-by-case basis, depending upon the particular facts. Legal counsel should be sought as appropriate.

Select federal non-discrimination laws include but are not limited to:

* Age Discrimination in Employment Act (ADEA) and Older Workers Benefit Protection Act (OWBPA).

* Americans With Disabilities Act and the ADA Amendments Act (ADA).

* Employee Retirement Income Security Act (ERISA).

* Equal Pay Act (EPA).

* Fair Labor Standards Act (FLSA).

* Family and Medical Leave Act (FMLA).

* Genetic Information Nondiscrimination Act (GINA).

* Health Insurance Portability and Accountability Act (HIPAA).

* Immigration Reform and Control Act (IRCA).

* National Labor Relations Act (NLRA).

* Occupational Safety and Health Act (OSHA).

* Patient Protection and Affordable Care Act (ACA).

* Pregnancy Discrimination Act (PDA).

* Title VII of the Civil Rights Act of 1964 and the Civil Rights Act of 1991 (Title VII).

* Uniformed Services Employment and Reemployment Rights Act (USERRA).

Related Websites

* Equal Employment Opportunity Commission (*www.eeoc.gov*).

    * ADEA; OWBPA; ADA; EPA; GINA; PDA, Title VII.

* Department of Labor Wage and Hour Division (*www.dol.gov/whd*).

    * FMLA; FLSA.

* Department of Labor Employee Benefits Security Administration (*www.dol.gov/ebsa*).

    * ERISA; HIPAA; ACA.

* Department of Labor (*www.dol.gov/compli-ance/laws/comp-osha.htm*).

    * OSHA.

* Department of Labor Veterans Employment and Training Services (*www.dol.gov/vets*).

  * USERRA.

* National Labor Relations Board (*www.nlrb.gov*).

  * NLRA.

* United States Citizenship and Immigration Services (*www.uscis.gov*).

  * IRCA.

Spiral of Disrespect

Micro-inequities
Subtle messages which can be offensive or devaluing

Discrimination or Harassment
Unlawful Behavior – if based on protected characteristics

Bullying
Generally verbal abuse

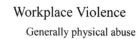

Workplace Violence
Generally physical abuse

Preventing Harassment— Managers' Guide

Although some of the information in this guide is specific to workplace harassment, it can serve as guiding principles for preventing other types of disruptive workplace behavior. Follow your organization's policies and enforce the policies and the rules.

✳ Immediately document observed or reported incidents of harassment.

✳ Notify human resources immediately.

If an employee says that he or she will handle the incident and does not want you to disclose it, you must advise that this is not an option. (The organization is obligated to investigate once it has knowledge of the alleged discrimination/harassment.)

✳ Remain neutral. Do not take sides.

✳ Maintain confidentiality.

Set a positive tone and example through your own actions and behaviors.

✳ Be mindful of behavior, language, and social interactions.

✳ Be respectful of others' personal space.

Be open to discussing the issue of harassment or other types of disruptive behaviors.

✳ Distribute copies of the policies when requested by management.

✳ Remind employees that discriminatory/harassing behaviors or remarks, or any other disrespectful behaviors or remarks, do not belong in the workplace.

Be actively alert for inappropriate workplace behavior. Treat it seriously.

* Act quickly. Don't put it off.

* Address improper conduct if you see it happening.

* Don't ignore it; it won't go away.

* Remember that, as a supervisor, if you knew or should have known of conduct that potentially could be harassment or discrimination, the company is liable to show that immediate and appropriate corrective action was taken.

Workplace Harassment—Employee Rights & Responsibilities

You have the right to work in an environment free from harassment or other disruptive behavior. Along with that right, goes the responsibility to assure your rights and those of your coworkers are protected. Though some of the information in this guide is specific to workplace harassment, it can serve as guiding principles for preventing other types of disruptive workplace behavior.

* Be an up-stander, not a by-stander. Speak up against potentially offensive and disruptive behavior. Even if you are an impartial observer, you have the right and responsibility to speak up.

* Describe the behavior that offends you.

* Explain the impact. Provide enough information so the offender understands the impact of the behavior on you and others.

* Let the individual know that the behavior is unwanted and you are asking for it to stop.

* If someone finds your behavior offensive or disruptive, don't get defensive. Listen for understanding and clarity.

* If the behavior continues, report it according to company policy.

* Be sensitive to the feelings, values, opinions, and attitudes of fellow employees.

* Recognize that harassment, sexual or otherwise, is seen through the eye of the beholder.

* Do not assume that coworkers enjoy hearing comments about their appearance, stories about your "love life," being touched, propositioned, or subjected to jokes of a sexual nature.

* Document details of incidents, including time, place, circumstances, and witnesses.

* Offer support to victims and intervene on their behalf.

* If you have any doubts about your own conduct, ask yourself: "Is it respectful?" Remember that respect is also in the eye of the beholder.

Sample Conflict Resolution Policy

Here is what you might want to include in a conflict resolution policy (not intended to be all-inclusive):

Purpose of the policy

Problems, misunderstandings, and frustrations may arise in the workplace. It is [insert organization's name]'s intent to be responsive to its employees and their concerns. The purpose of this policy is to provide a quick, effective, and consistently applied method for a nonsupervisory employee to present his/her concerns to management and have those concerns internally resolved. Therefore, if you are confronted with a problem, you may use the following procedure to resolve or clarify your concerns.

Procedures

Step 1. Discuss with supervisor.

Initially, you should bring your concern or complaint to your immediate supervisor. If the complaint involves your supervisor, you should meet with his/her supervisor to discuss the problem within five days of the date the incident occurred.

The supervisor should respond in writing to you within five days of the meeting.

Step 2. Written complaint and decision.

If the discussion with your supervisor (or his/her supervisor) does not resolve the problem to the mutual satisfaction of you and the supervisor, or if the supervisor does not respond, you may submit a written complaint to your department's director or vice president. You may request help from Human Resources to write your complaint if needed. The director or vice president should forward a copy of the complaint to Human Resources.

The complaint should outline the problem and the date it occurred, suggestions on how to resolve the issue, and the response from the supervisor along with the date you met with the supervisor.

Upon receipt of the formal complaint, the director or vice president must schedule a meeting with you within five business days and should issue a decision within five days of the date of the meeting.

Step 3. Appeal of the decision.

If you are not satisfied with the decision of the director or vice president, you may, within five business days, appeal the decision in writing to the HR Department.

The HR Department may call a meeting with everyone involved to facilitate a resolution or may refer the complaint to a review committee.

The parties involved in the complaint should refrain from discussing it with anyone with the exception of the HR Department, in order to preserve the integrity of any investigation that may be necessary.

If an employee fails to appeal from one level to the next level of this procedure within the time limits previously set forth, the problem will be considered settled on the basis of the last decision and the problem will not be subject to further consideration.

[Organization name] reserves the right to impose appropriate disciplinary action for any conduct it considers to be disruptive or inappropriate. The circumstances of each situation may differ, and the level of disciplinary action may also vary depending on factors such as the nature of the offense, whether it is repeated, the employee's work record, and the impact of the conduct on the organization.

No employee will be subject to retaliation for filing a complaint under this policy.

Notes

Introduction

1. Lynne Eisaguirre, *The Power of a Good Fight* (Indianapolis, IN: Alpha, A Pearson Education, 2002), p. xiii.

Chapter 1

1. Sharon Armstrong, *The Essential Performance Review Handbook* (Franklin Lakes, NJ: Career Press, 2010), p. 109.

2. Richard Y. Chang, *Mastering Change Management* (San Francisco: Jossey-Bass Pfeiffer, 1994), p. 5.

3. Lee Gardenswartz and Anita Rowe, *Diverse Teams at Work* (Alexandria, VA: SHRM, 2003), p. 133.

4. Susan Mulligan, "Wisdom of the Ages," *HR Magazine*, November 2014, p. 24.

5. Patrick Lencioni, *The Advantage* (Hoboken, NJ: Jossey-Bass, 2012), p. 38.

Chapter 2

1. Marilyn Loden, *Implementing Diversity* (Burr Ridge, IL: Irwin Professional Publishing, 1996), pp. 14–15.

2. *www.bls.gov/cps/demographics.htm.*

3. *www.forbes.com/sites/rawnshah/2011/04/20/working-with-five-generations-in-the-workplace/.*

4. Elizabeth F. Fideler, *Women Still At Work: Professionals Over Sixty and On the Job* (Lanham, MD: Rowman & Littlefield Publishers, Inc., 2012), p. 46.

5. Douglas Stone, Bruce Patton, and Sheila Heen, *Difficult Conversations: How to Discuss What Matters Most* (New York, NY: Penguin Books, 1999), pp. 31–34.

6. Dana Wilkie, "Rooting Out Hidden Bias," *HR Magazine*, December 2014, p. 25.

7. Steve L. Robbins, *What If? Short Stories to Spark Diversity Dialogue* (Mountain View, CA: Davies-Black Publishing, 2008), p. 75.

8. Robbins, p. 58.

9. Robbins, p. 82.

10. Robbins, p. xiii.

11. Stone, p. 176.

12. William Ury, *The Power of a Positive No* (New York, NY: Bantam Books, 2004), p. 82.

Chapter 3

1. Patrick Lencioni, *The Advantage* (San Francisco: Jossey-Bass, 2012), p. 21.

2. Lee Gardenswartz and Anita Rowe, *Diverse Teams at Work* (Alexandria, VA: SHRM, 2003), p 156.

3. Stephen Covey, *The Seven Habits of Highly Effective People* (New York, NY: Free Press, 1989), p. 248.

4. Lee Gardenswartz and Anita Rowe, *Diverse Teams at Work* (Alexandria, VA: SHRM, 2003), p 75.

5. Lencioni, p. 38.

6. Lencioni, p. 27.

7. Daniel Goleman, *Working with Emotional Intelligence* (New York, NY: Bantam Books, 2004), p. 219.

8. Robert Heller and Tim Hindle, *The Essential Manager's Handbook* (New York, NY: DK Publishing, 1998), p. 363.

Chapter 4

1. Michael Watkins, Subject Advisor, *The Essentials of Negotiations* (Boston: Harvard Business School Press, 2005), p. 65.

2. Kerry Patterson, Joseph Grenny, Ron McMillan, and Al Switzler, *Crucial Conversations, Tools for Talking When Stakes are High* (New York, NY: McGraw Hill, 2011), p. 20.

3. Barbara Mitchell and Cornelia Gamlem, *The Big Book of HR* (Pompton Plains, NJ: Career Press, 2011), p. 198.

4. Perry Zeus and Suzanne Skiffington, *The Coaching at Work Toolkit, A Complete Guide to Techniques and Practices* (New York, NY: McGraw Hill, 2003), pp.164–165.

5. Patterson, Grenny, McMillan, and Switzler, p. 21.

6. Mitchell and Gamlem, p. 197.

7. Mitchell and Gamlem, p. 199.

8. Douglas Stone, Bruce Patton, and Sheila Heen, *Difficult Conversations: How to Discuss What Matters Most* (New York, NY: Penguin Books, 2010), pp. 12–13.

9. Stone, Patton, and Heen, pp. 18–19.

10. Kerry Patterson, Joseph Grenny, Ron McMillan, and Al Switzler, *Crucial Confrontations, Tools for Resolving Broken Promises, Violated Expectations, and Bad Behavior* (New York, NY: McGraw Hill, 2005), p. 34.

Chapter 5

1. Daniel Goleman, *Working with Emotional intelligence* (New York, NY: Bantam Books, 1998), p. 140.

2. Eisaguirre, Lynne, *The Power of a Good Fight* (Indianapolis, IN: Alpha Books, 2002), p.158.

3. Jennifer Nycz-Connor, *Washington Business Journal*, November 4, 2014, p. 54.

4. *www.goodreads.com/quotes/633610-the-most-important-thing-in-communication-is-hearing-what-isn-t.*

5. Mitchell and Gamlem, *The Big Book of HR*, p. 198.

6. Mark Goulston, *Just Listen: Discover the Secret to Getting Through to Absolutely Everyone,* (New York, NY: AMACOM, 2010), p. 39.

7. Eisaguirre, p. 165.

8. *www.brainyquote.com/quotes/authors/j/john_marshall.html.*

Chapter 6

1. Kerry Patterson, Joseph Grenny, Ron McMillan, and Al Switzler, *Crucial Conversations, Tools for Talking When Stakes are High* (New York, NY: McGraw Hill, 2011), p. 108.

2. Patterson, et al., p. 119.

3. Patterson, et al., p. 128.

4. Mitchell and Gamlem, p. 190.

5. Ury, p. 68.

6. Mitchell and Gamlem, pp. 192–193.

7. Sharon Armstrong and Barbara Mitchell, *The Essential HR Handbook* (Franklin Lakes, NJ: Career Press, 2008), pp. 64–65.

8. *https://hbr.org/2015/02/how-to-coach-according-to-5-great-sports-coaches.*

9. *www.mindtools.com/pages/article/newLDR_44.htm.*

10. Gary Seigel, PhD, *The Mouth Trap* (Franklin Lakes, NJ: Career Press, 2008), pp. 130–132.

Chapter 7

1. Roger Fisher and William Ury, *Getting to Yes* (New York: Penguin Books, 1991), p. 15.

2. Tim Ursiny, *The Coward's Guide to Conflict* (Naperville, IL: Sourcebooks, Inc., 2003), p. 137.

3. William Ury, *The Power of a Positive No* (New York, NY: Bantam Books, 2004), pp. 30–31.

4. Rosamund Stone Zander and Benjamin Zander, *The Art of Possibility* (New York: Penguin Group, 2000), p. 15.

5. Fisher and Ury, pp. 85–86.

6. Ury, pp. 114–115.

7. Michael Watkins, Subject Advisor, *The Essentials of Negotiations* (Boston: Harvard Business School Press, 2005), p. 112.

8. Mitchell and Gamlem, p. 205.

9. Mitchell and Gamlem, p. 109.

Chapter 8

1. Mitchell and Gamlem, p. 219.
2. Eisaguirre, p. 58.
3. Mitchell and Gamlem, p. 220.

Chapter 9

1. Douglas Stone, Bruce Patton, and Sheila Heen, *Difficult Conversations: How to Discuss What Matters Most* (New York, NY: Penguin Books, 2010), p.150.
2. Mitchell and Gamlem, p. 230.
3. *www.eeoc.gov/laws/types/sexual_harassment. cfm.*

Chapter 10

1. http://www.eeoc.gov/laws/types/harassment. cfm.
2. Dennis A. Davis, PhD, "Bullying, Harassment, and Violence: What's Atmosphere Got to Do With It?" *Ogletree Deakins, The Employment Law Authority*, October/November 2014, p. 4.
3. Davis, p. 4.
4. Tom Larkin and Jean Marie Johnson, "What's in a Micro-Message?" *www.communicoltd.com/ pages/1017_are_microinequities_damaging_ your_workplace_.cfm.*
5. Patterson, et al., p. 98.
6. *www.bullyingstatistics.org/content/workplace- bullying.html.*

7. Davis, p. 5.

8. Beverly Langford, *The Etiquette Edge* (New York, NY: AMACOM, 2005), p. 35.

9. Langford, p. 40.

10. http://www2.ucsc.edu/title9-sh/intent.htm.

11. Stone, et al., p. 46.

12. Stone, et al., p. 53.

13. Chapter 11

14. Mitchell and Gamlem, p. 171.

15. Mitchell and Gamlem, p. 209.

16. Mitchell and Gamlem, p. 209.

17. Mitchell and Gamlem, p. 210.

18. Mitchell and Gamlem, p. 208.

19. Mitchell and Gamlem, p. 229.

20. Scott Eblin, *Overworked and Overwhelmed* (Hoboken, NJ: John Wiley & Sons, Inc., 2014), p. 8.

21. Eblin, p. 18.

22. Mitchell and Gamlem, p. 158.

23. Mitchell and Gamlem, p. 106.

BIBLIOGRAPHY

Armstrong, Sharon. *The Essential Performance Review Handbook*. Franklin Lakes,NJ: Career Press, 2010.

Armstrong, Sharon, and Barbara Mitchell. *The Essential HR Handbook*. Franklin Lakes, NJ: Career Press, 2008.

Covey, Stephen. *The Seven Habits of Highly Effective People*. New York, NY: Free Press, 1989.

Crowe, Sandra. *Since Strangling Isn't an Option*. New York, NY: The Berkley Publishing Group, 1999.

Eblin, Scott. *Overworked and Overwhelmed*. Hoboken, NJ: John Wiley & Sons, 2014.

Eisaguirre, Lynne. *The Power of a Good Fight*. Indianapolis, IN: Alpha Books, 2006.

Fisher, Roger, and William Ury. *Getting to Yes: Negotiating Agreement Without Giving In*. New York, NY: Penguin Books, 2011.

Gardenswartz, Lee, PhD, and Anita Rowe, PhD. *Diverse Teams at Work*. Alexandria, VA: Society for Human Resource Management, Alexandria, VA, 2003.

Goleman, Daniel. *Working with Emotional Intelligence*. New York, NY: Bantam Books, 2004.

Goulston, Mark. *Just Listen: Discover the Secret to Getting Through to Absolutely Everyone*. New York, NY: AMACOM, 2010.

Heller, Robert, and Tim Hindle. *The Essential Manager's Handbook*. New York, NY: DK Publishing, 1998.

Langford, Beverly. *The Etiquette Edge: The Unspoken Rules for Business Success*. New York, NY: AMACOM, 2005.

Lencioni, Patrick. *The Advantage*. Hoboken, NJ: Jossey-Bass, 2012.

Mitchell, Barbara, and Cornelia Gamlem. *The Big Book of HR*. Pompton Plains, NJ: Career Press, 2012.

Mulligan, Susan. "Wisdom of the Ages." *HR Magazine*, November, 2014.

Patterson, Kerry, Joseph Grenny, Ron McMillian, and Al Switzier. *Crucial Conversations*. New York, NY: McGraw Hill, 2011.

———. *Crucial Confrontations*. New York, NY: McGraw Hill, 2005.

Pink, Daniel H. *Drive: The Surprising Truth About What Motivates Us*. New York: Riverhead Hardcover, A Penguin Group Imprint, 2009.

Robbins, Steve L. *What If? Short Stories to Spark Diversity Dialogue*. Mountain View, CA: Davies-Black Publishing, 2008.

Seigel, Gary. *The Mouth Trap*. Franklin Lakes, NJ: Career Press, 2008.

Stone, Douglas, Bruce Patton, and Sheila Heen. *Difficult Conversations: How to Discuss What Matters Most*. New York, NY: Penguin Books, 2010.

Trompenaars, Fons, and Charles Hampden-Turner. *Riding the Waves of Culture*. New York, NY: McGraw-Hill, 2012.

Ursiny, Tim, PhD. *The Coward's Guide to Conflict*. Naperville, IL: Sourcebooks, Inc., 2003.

Index

ABOUT THE AUTHORS

In 2010, Career Press approached Barbara Mitchell about writing another book. She had previously co-authored *The Essential HR Handbook* with Sharon Armstrong. When the proposal was accepted, Barbara reached out to her colleague Cornelia Gamlem, with the offer to coauthor *The Big Book of HR*. Drawing on their collective experience, Barbara and Cornelia produced a great resource for HR professionals, managers, business leaders, small-business owners, and anyone who has to manage people. A writing partnership was born. Since the publication of *The Big Book of HR* in 2012, Barbara and Cornelia continue to collaborate on a weekly blog, *Making People Matter*. In 2014, Career Press approached them once again about writing *The Essential Workplace Conflict Handbook*. They are likely to write more books in the future.

Both Barbara and Cornelia are influencers to the HR and business communities. They are frequent speakers to business groups and have been quoted in major publications including *The Wall Street Journal*, *Financial Times*, *Fortune*, and *The New York Times*. Since writing *The Big Book of HR*, they have been interviewed in major markets around the country.

Barbara Mitchell is an author, speaker, and the managing partner of The Mitchell Group, a human resources and organizational development consulting practice. She consults with a wide variety of clients on issues around people—helping them successfully hire, develop, engage, and retain the best talent available. Most of her HR career was spent in senior leadership positions with Marriott International, Human Genome Sciences, and as co-owner and principal of The Millennium Group International, LLC.

She entered the HR profession after gaining a strong business foundation and says, "Working in HR was like coming home. I'd found what I was meant to do!"

Barbara has actively given back to the HR profession in a variety of ways. She served on the board of directors of the Employment Management Association, a professional emphasis group of the Society for Human Resource Management (SHRM), and has been president of several SHRM chapters. She is a passionate supporter of the SHRM Foundation.

She is a graduate of North Park University, Chicago, IL, with a degree in history and political science. She has taken graduate level business courses at UCLA, the University of Denver, and Loyola University.

Barbara serves on the executive committee of the board of directors of the Northern Virginia Habitat for Humanity affiliate and is a video presenter/docent at the Smithsonian's American Art Museum.

Cornelia Gamlem, SPHR, is an author, consultant, and speaker. She is founder and president of the GEMS Group ltd., a management consulting firm that offers human resources and business solutions. Prior to founding the firm, she served in a senior HR leadership role with a Fortune 500 IT services company with a global presence. She likes to say that she's been in HR since "God was a girl."

Cornelia has served on national task forces that influenced public policy and testified before the Equal Employment Opportunity Commission on three occasions. She served on SHRM's National Board of Directors, chaired its Workplace Diversity Committee, and served on its Global Forum Board of Directors. She has supported HR professionals by serving as an instructor at a number of colleges in the Washington, DC metropolitan area. She has written many articles and white papers for professional and industry publications.

She is a graduate of Marymount University, where she earned a master's degree in Human Resource management, and California State University, Sacramento, where she earned her undergraduate degree in business administration. She achieved Life Certification as Senior Professional in Human Resources (SPHR) from the Human Resource Certification Institute (HRCI).

The authors can be reached at *www.essentialwork-placeconflicthandbook.com* or *www.bigbookofhr.com*.